An Artist's Guide to the Law

Law and Legal Concepts Every Artist, Performer, Writer, or Other Creative Person Ought to Know

An Artist's Guide to the Law

Law and Legal Concepts Every Artist, Performer, Writer, or Other Creative Person Ought to Know

Richard Amada

Contents

Acknowledgments

The author wishes to thank and acknowledge the contributions of those who helped to make this book possible. It was my publisher Ron Pullins (Focus Publishing) who first suggested the project to me and allowed me the opportunity to put my knowledge of the law and my knowledge of the arts to one single, textual purpose. That text profited substantially from the editing of Hailey Klein, associate editor and acquisitions, and Cindy Zawalich, editorial and production assistant. I was further advantaged to have had attorney/playwright Regina Ramsay, Esq., review, comment, and make suggestions regarding an earlier draft. It was my privilege to have benefitted from the expertise of these people. Finally, to friends and colleagues who, while this writing was being undertaken, invited me to participate in one project or another—artistic or otherwise—only to hear me say, "I'd love to, but I'm writing my book now," I gratefully acknowledge their understanding and support. To all mentioned above, I thank you most sincerely.

Introduction

"The first thing we do, let's kill all the lawyers."

Oh, that Billy Shakespeare! What a cut-up!

There's actually a good deal of argument over whether the Bard's oft quoted line from *Henry VI, Part II* was supposed to be a lawyer joke or an homage to the profession that was best equipped to stop the dastardly anarchists in the play who were illegally trying to take over the government. Like so much else that gets written down, there are various ways to interpret the words, and, since Shakespeare's not around to ask anymore, people are likely to read into the line whatever meaning they like. Of course, your interpretation might just be tinged by whether your own personal experiences with lawyers have been good ones or bad ones. Every client likes his lawyer when the case has been won. There tends to be less fondness for the attorney when the case is lost. So, if we want to know what Shakespeare really thought of lawyers, maybe we should find out if he was ever successfully sued.

At this point I should probably mention that I happen to *be* a lawyer. That said, in the interest of full disclosure, I'll just state for the record that I haven't a clue what Shakespeare really thought of people in my profession. What I can say is that, despite my admiration for his wizardry with dramatic poetry, he obviously was not trained in the law. How do I know this? *Exhibit A*—Act IV, Scene 1 from *The Merchant of Venice*:

Plaintiff Shylock is denied the pound of flesh he's entitled to under the gory terms of his loan agreement with defendant Antonio because of a supposed loophole in the contract that makes no provision for any blood being spilled while the flesh is being carved. The judge warns Shylock that, while he can take a knife to Antonio's flesh, if he "dost shed one drop" of blood Shylock will have everything he owns confiscated as punishment for violating the letter of the agreement. Apparently, in Shakespeare's version of jurisprudence, a contract was an excruciatingly precise thing that required absolutely explicit clauses for an exacting definition of all terms. In short, if it ain't on the page, it ain't in the agreement.

However, contract law doesn't really work that way. It's not nearly so anal retentive a field of law that it doesn't allow for certain implicit elements of a contract. Some components of an agreement are naturally implied. For example, if I contract with you to sell you a gallon of lemonade, it's implicit in that contract that the lemonade will come in a container of some sort. I can't simply dump the lemonade on your head and then claim, because a container wasn't specified in the agreement, that I've fulfilled my part of the bargain. No court would uphold that argument. If you're buying a liquid, unless you've specifically stated that you want it dumped on your head, you've a right to expect that the agreement's implied requirement is that it be delivered to you in a container.

The same would hold true for the "drop of blood" loophole. If you contract with a surgeon to perform an appendectomy, you can't later sue that surgeon because the surgical consent agreement didn't explicitly state that the surgeon was allowed to draw blood when the incision was made. It's quite obviously implied that any cutting of flesh will naturally produce bleeding. If Antonio agreed to allow Shylock to cut into his skin, he implicitly agreed to allow for bleeding to occur. Under the terms of the agreement, Shylock would not have breached the contract by causing Antonio to bleed while exacting his pound of flesh.

The more likely and stronger argument against upholding the macabre contract of Shylock and Antonio is one that Shakespeare didn't even bother to mention. Specifically, a contract won't be upheld if the exercising of its terms is against public policy. Murder was illegal in Shakespeare's day as well as today, and carving a pound of flesh out of Antonio's heart (which was Shylock's plan) would certainly have killed him. That, alone, was enough to void the contract. (Think of it this way. I couldn't sue somebody for breaching an agreement to commit armed robbery for me. What's the judge going to do?—order someone to stick up a bank in order to fulfill the contract?)

Now I don't hold those little nitpicks against the Bard. After all, the law wasn't his field. He was an artist, and most artists aren't legal scholars. However, a writer, performer, visual artist, or other creative person, who has little to no knowledge regarding the legalities and illegalities that govern these professions, is an artist who can get into a world of trouble without even realizing it's happening—that is, until it's too late and the lawyers have to be called in to do a potentially costly cleanup of the mess. Much better to bone up on some basic principles of law that allow the artist to avoid potential legal pitfalls. That's where this book comes in.

An Artist's Guide to the Law is written especially for creative people in the arts and entertainment fields, whether professional or aspiring, who want a general overview of key aspects of the law that relate to their artistic endeavors. In the following chapters, I'll attempt to explain in plain, simple English the answers to some basic, legal questions I believe every artist ought to know—namely:

- What does the artist own?
- What is the artist selling?
- What can and can't the artist use?
- What is the artist allowed and not allowed to say?
- How does the artist protect intellectual property?
- What contracts does the artist make?
- What happens to art when the artist no longer possesses it?

It should be noted that my use of the word, "artist," is merely a shorthand reference for all creative people in the arts and entertainment industries. I'll be using the term throughout the book, and, unless I specifically reference a particular type of artist, you may assume that I'm speaking generally about all types of artists.

Ahem…Now comes the big disclaimer. Yes, that's right. You can't talk to a lawyer without getting a legal disclaimer.

IMPORTANT. PLEASE READ THIS.

THE INFORMATION IN THIS BOOK IS NOT,
NOR IS IT INTENDED TO BE, LEGAL ADVICE.

Application of the law is extremely fact specific. For example, you're not allowed to go through a red light…unless you happen to be driving a fire engine at the time and you're racing to a three-alarm blaze. See how a small change in the facts can make a huge difference? That being the case, absolutely nothing in this book can or should be taken as legal advice for anyone's specific situation. This book is meant to be a general guide to the law as it relates to artists. Its purpose is to help you understand, plan, and function as an artist in a world full of laws that directly affect you. If you have a particular legal issue that's specific to you, personally, there simply is no substitute for consulting a lawyer as your professional legal counsel. Although I'm a lawyer, I'm not *your* lawyer just because you're reading my book.

Additionally, everything in this book must be qualified with the understanding: first, that it is not meant to be an exhaustive treatise on any of the topics discussed within its pages, but, rather, it's a general overview of key legal concepts important to artists; and, second, that it is written from the standpoint of general American jurisprudence. That is, the legal concepts discussed within this text are those common to the law as it is interpreted in the United States of America. Other countries often have different laws and practices that cannot realistically be covered sufficiently in this book. Therefore, no attempt is being made here to analyze how a law might apply if you're operating in a non-American jurisdiction. What's more, even within the United States, laws and rulings on laws can vary by state, and they can change over time. This is why it's vitally important that, if you've got a legal problem and you're not certain how the law applies to you, you should contact an attorney for guidance.

So, now that we have that out of the way, we stand on the very brink of launching into a discussion of all the legal stuff that's the whole reason you started reading this in the first place. But, before we do, perhaps you're asking yourself a few questions, like: Who is this guy? Why is he writing this particular book on this particular topic? And what does he know about what an artist's work is all about?

The answer's simple. In addition to being a practicing attorney, I'm also an artist, myself. Among my artistic callings, I'm a writer, an actor, a musician, a composer, a director—sometimes professionally and sometimes just for the love of the art. Much of what I'll be sharing with you in this book is information that I, myself, have researched and utilized in my own artistic endeavors. I believe being an artist gives me certain insights that help me better understand what's important to other people in the arts, and I like to think that makes me a better lawyer when I'm counseling my clients who are artists. Additionally, a sheer fascination with this area of the law has led me to ask myself various questions and seek out the answers—or, at the very least, ponder the possibilities. I created an arts-and-the-law blog called *The Artful Jurist* (artfuljurist.com) specifically to allow me to ponder these things publicly for the benefit of others who might also be musing on similar topics. The questions that have been posed to me by those who have read the blog, and by those whom I have encountered in my own artistic ventures, have helped me discern what areas of the law are of greatest interest and importance to artists. Based on that, I've written this book as an attempt to tell artists what they want to know and what they need to know.

Knowledge, it is said, is power. I believe knowing how the law works in relation to my art makes me a more powerful artist. I hope it does the same for you.

~ Rich Amada

What Does the Artist Own?

When you're talking about law for the arts and entertainment fields, more often than not you're talking about one of two areas of law: property law and contract law. The first concerns ownership rights—who owns what and what they're allowed to do with it. The second involves the transaction end of the business—the transferring of some or all of those property rights from the creator to someone else. That "someone else" we'll call "the buyer." At the very least, we'll assume it's someone the artist hopes will help advance the artist's career through some sort of agreement involving the purchasing, exhibiting, performing, or otherwise presenting of the artist's work. While I know that artists typically prefer to focus on the aesthetic rather than the commercial part of their calling, don't discount the importance of the buyer in this whole process. Unless your plan is to keep your art solely to yourself, at some point a buyer is necessary if you desire to share your artistic vision and talents with the world at large. So, when that time comes, it can't hurt for you to know a thing or two about contract law and the rules that govern the business of art.

And, yes, yes!—we'll get to that contract stuff! I know you're just champing at the bit to ink that big deal! But, before you can sell something, you first need to know what it is you actually *own* that's available for selling. Perhaps that seems like a ridiculously simple thing that shouldn't require any explanation whatsoever. However, if you know anything at all about the law, you ought to know that the law specializes in making even some of the simplest things far more complex than you might ever have imagined. So we begin our discussion with a little basic property law.

The Bundle of Sticks: Property Law Basics

This is a concept that most if not all law students encounter when they begin their studies of property. It's the so-called *Bundle of Sticks*, a concept that's designed to provide a comprehensible example of how property law works. It goes like this:

Imagine, if you will, that someone possesses a bundle of sticks. Someone else sees it and comments...

"Hey, Leslie, that's a mighty fine bundle of sticks you've got there. I wish I had some sticks like that."

(One can only assume that this representational example comes from some distant past epoch when sticks were considered a marketable commodity much in demand. But let's try not to get hung up on the details here, shall we?)

Leslie responds...

"Well, Ron, I need the dry, brown sticks for my fire. But, if you'll let me have a few of your rocks, I'll let you take the moist, green sticks."

The deal has been struck, and Ron gleefully removes from the bundle only the green sticks, leaving the brown ones in Leslie's possession.

This is the concept of divisible property rights at its most elemental. Leslie possessed one bundle, but within that bundle were a number of individual sticks, each one severable from the rest. Leslie could just as easily have told Ron that he could have only those sticks that were less than twenty inches long, or only those sticks that were of a particular type of wood, or only those sticks that had the bark still on them. It's Leslie's bundle, and she's free to give it all away or to distribute its separate components however she likes. In this case, she chose to give Ron the green sticks because the moist, green ones don't make good firewood.

Of course, there was no mention in the agreement between them as to what's supposed to happen when Ron's newly acquired green sticks eventually dry out and turn brown. If the sticks are no longer green, does their ownership revert back to Leslie?...

"Hey, Ron, I said you could only have the green sticks."

"I only took the green ones."

"Yeah, well, those sticks are brown."

"They were green when I took 'em."

"Well, they're brown now, so fork over!"

"No way! We had a deal!"

Well, you can see where this is heading. Thanks to the imprecise nature of the transaction's terms, Ron and Leslie are about to lawyer up for a massive court battle in what undoubtedly back then would have been considered the trial of the century. See?—Didn't I tell you the law can make even simple things complicated?

But, putting aside their dispute for the moment, imagine now that something you own is represented by a bundle of sticks and that each stick represents one individual piece of the whole. You can sell or give away all of the pieces or just certain pieces, reserving the others for yourself, or you could transfer some pieces to one person and other pieces to someone else—and, if you haven't yet given away all the pieces, you could still transfer some other pieces to a third, fourth, fifth person, and so on. That's easy enough to visualize when the object is a bundle of sticks or something else where there are physically a number of separate pieces that compose the whole of the bundle. But what about property that doesn't come in a lot of little, distinct pieces? What about something that's physically only one piece?

Let's take, for example, a photograph. A photo, assuming it has been printed only once on a piece of photographic paper, is a single, tangible object you're able to hold in your hand, put in an album, or mount on the wall. If you took the photo using your own camera, it's your photo to do with as you want. If you want to give the print (or sell it) to someone else, that's your call. However, if you give the print to another person, have you given away all the "sticks" in that photo's bundle? The answer is—not necessarily. Even though the print, itself, is only a single piece, the property rights (the individual "sticks") that go with it are several pieces. For example, there's the right to publish the photo in a book. Just because you give a friend a print of your photo doesn't mean you've given that friend the right to use that photo in your friend's new book. That's a property right that doesn't automatically transfer with the physical possession of a photo print. It's a property right that must be transferred *specifically*. Otherwise, it's a stick that remains in the photographer's bundle. The same holds true for the right to put the photo on the cover of a magazine, or the right to use the photo in an advertisement. It's the same for the right to duplicate the photo and sell it on posters, T-shirts, dishware, mugs, mouse pads, computer screensavers, what have you. Like Leslie's retained brown sticks, those are all separate rights that remain the property of the photographer until such time as the photographer gives them away.

You can apply the bundle of sticks philosophy to any creative work that is either a tangible object or a captured expression of creativity that's generally known as *intellectual property*. A work of art, whether it be a photograph, a song, a sculpture, a poem, a dance, or any of a horde of other possibilities, is a piece of property with many potential rights attached to it, and each right is one that can be individually assigned (sold or given away), retained, licensed, or bequeathed to heirs, irrespective of what's done with any of the other rights associated with the work.

Among the rights that go with works of art is the right to physically possess it. If you buy a painting, you expect to be able to take the painting home and hang it on your wall. On the other end of the same spectrum is the right to display the art without actually possessing it. When a play is produced by a theater company, the company doesn't actually buy the play. It just purchases the right to perform it for a given period of time at a particular location.

Another property right is the right to reproduce the art. As I said earlier, you might not want your friend to take the uninvited initiative of putting your photo in your friend's own book. (Perhaps you won't approve of the subject matter of the book or the way your photo is used in it. What's more, you might not think it fair of your friend to cash in on your creative genius while you get nothing in return.) But, if you grant your friend permission to use the photo in the book, you're also going to have to grant permission for your friend's publisher to reproduce the photo in every copy of the book that's printed. That doesn't mean you've given the photo away to your friend or the publisher, or that you've granted free license for anyone to reproduce the photo however they like. It just means that this particular right of reproduction has been granted for this particular book. Unless you also grant your friend exclusive use of the photo (yet another separate property right), you can still license its reproduction to anyone else you care to allow to use it.

Of course, marketing rights are a huge part of intellectual property transactions. *What* can be sold; *when* it can be sold; to *whom* it can be sold; *how* it can be sold—these are all property rights that can be specified with as much particularity as deemed necessary. *Where* something can be sold is quite often a property right that undergoes a lot of negotiation in intellectual property transactions. Coca Cola may have marketing clout in most of the world, but many companies don't, and, for that reason marketing rights are sometimes restricted by region.

Say, for example, you're a filmmaker contracting with a company—which we'll call Boffo American Films—for the distribution of your latest motion picture to the various movie theaters that will screen it. Now Boffo American may be tops in the United States for the distribution of feature films. However, its inroads into European markets might be slight, thus, making Boffo American a less than stellar choice as a distributor on the other side of the Atlantic. If you grant Boffo American worldwide distribution rights, then you're stuck with Boffo American even if it can't place your film in a single European theater. This being the case, you, the filmmaker, might be better off selling Boffo American the distribution rights only for the United States or North America while reserving the European distribution rights for someone else who might be able to do a lot more for you in that part of the world.

If you're wondering how many different property rights there can be in any given piece of property, I'd have to say it's only limited by your ability to think up different, non-conflicting property rights. If you assign the rights piecemeal, you can apportion them out as narrowly as you're able to convince the receiving party to accept them. Of course, the buyer isn't likely to agree to such a narrow slice of rights that he won't be able to utilize the property for its intended purpose. (There's no point to owning the right to distribute a film if that doesn't also come with the right to authorize the movie theaters to show the film to an audience.) That's why, unless *all the rights* are being assigned without exclusion, contracts for the purchase of and marketing of intellectual property are often lengthy. The buyer wants to be sure that the rights being purchased cover all the essential needs in all the possible ways the buyer envisions using that property. Hey, you wouldn't buy a car if it didn't come with an engine, would you?

Copyright Basics

Among the rights virtually every artist seems to inherently know he possesses are the protections we call *copyright*. However, many artists—if not most—have little to no knowledge of how copyright actually works. Misconceptions abound and misinformation gets passed around faster than a supermarket tabloid with headlines about Hollywood celebrities mating with space aliens. So we should take a little time to get to know this oh-so-important point of law.

What seems to be the most prevalent misconception out there is the notion that copyright is somehow a race to the Copyright Office registration desk. Those who subscribe to this school of thought are convinced that the first person to register a work becomes the copyright owner, regardless of whether or not that person actually was the originator of the work. In reality, nothing could be farther from the truth.

My assumption is that people tend to confuse copyright with patents. Getting a patent *is* a race to the registration desk. The first person to submit to the U.S. Patent and Trademark Office an application for a patent on an original, novel invention is the person who will be awarded the patent for that creation. From that point forward, for the duration of the patent, that first applicant will own the exclusive right to control the manufacture and marketing of the patented invention.

Attaining a copyright works nothing like that.

It used to be that, under American law, you had to register your creative work with the Copyright Office to claim the copyright. But Congress changed the law with the passage of the Copyright Act of 1976, and, for all works created on or after January 1, 1978, copyright takes effect immediately and automatically upon the work's creation. The official statute, taken from the Act, reads:

> *Copyright protection subsists, in accordance with this title, in original works of authorship fixed in any tangible medium of expression, now known or later developed, from which they can be perceived, reproduced, or otherwise communicated, either directly or with the aid of a machine or device.*[1]

That means the moment you have recorded your original, creative work in or on something that can then be shown to or played for another person, you've done everything you need to do to claim the copyright on it. It's automatic, without you having to file any sort of official registration. Official registration with the Copyright Office is still a good idea if you're putting the work out into the marketplace or shopping it around where people will be encountering it or passing it about. In such situations, it doesn't hurt to have the fact of your copyright's existence made into a public record, and

---

1   For those of you who want the official statutory citation from the United States Code, it's 17 U.S.C. § 102(a). The full text of the Copyright Act is available on the United States Copyright Office's website, www.copyright.gov.

doing so is simple. Copyright registration can now be accomplished either through the mail using the application forms available from the Copyright Office or through electronic registration at the Copyright Office's website.[2] However, even if you never apply for official registration, someone else can't just swipe your creation, rush it down to the Copyright Office, and steal the copyright out from under you. If you're the original creator, the copyright belongs to you, with or without the participation of the Copyright Office.

Now I know some of you are already starting to fret over the above statutory language that says copyright is accorded to "original works of authorship." I can hear some of you saying, "Rich, I'm an *artist*, but I'm not an *author*! I don't even write a grocery list!" Well, fear not. The same clause of the same statute defines "authorship" far more broadly than you, yourself, might ordinarily define the term. Again, quoting from the Act:
Works of authorship include the following categories:

- Literary works
- Musical works, including any accompanying words
- Dramatic works, including any accompany music
- Pantomimes and choreographic works
- Pictorial, graphic, and sculptural works
- Motion pictures and other audiovisual works
- Sound recordings
- Architectural works

These general categories are meant to be interpreted very broadly. The Copyright Office's own website suggests, for example, that, maps might fall under the "pictorial, graphic, and sculptural works" category, and the Office further suggests that computer programs may be considered "literary works."

The fact is that copyright's sphere of protection has grown throughout history to incorporate more types of works, including those of new

---

2   The web address is www.copyright.gov/register. The website contains all the information you need to register your work, including the application forms, current registration fees, and the requirements for depositing a sample of the work being registered. If you don't have access to the Internet, the telephone number for the Copyright Office is (202) 707-3000, and its mailing address is U.S. Copyright Office, 101 Independence Ave., S.E., Washington, DC 20559-6000.

technologies. We can trace our copyright heritage as far back as the Statute of Anne, adopted in Great Britain in 1709 as a means of protecting authors and their publishers from unauthorized copying of their books. Later, America adopted its own statutory protections for creative works. Our copyright law springs directly from the Constitution. Article I, Section 8, Clause 8 specifically grants to Congress the power "To promote the Progress of Science and useful Arts, by securing for limited Times to Authors and Inventors the exclusive Right to their respective Writings and Discoveries."

Now I know some of you are already thinking to yourselves, "There they go with that 'Authors' and 'Writings' stuff again! We told you, we're *artists* but we're not all *writers*!" Yes, I appreciate that, and, apparently, so did the people who wrote the Constitution. Because when the Congress enacted its first copyright act in 1790 (and keep in mind that many of those who were in that first Congress were people who also helped draft the Constitution a few years before), the act specifically enumerated protection for maps, charts, and books. While that hardly encompasses all creative works, at least Congress's incorporation of maps and charts into the legislation suggests that the 'Writings' they envisioned as being entitled to copyright protection were more than just prose and poetry. That they didn't happen to think to themselves back in the 18th century that the law might someday also need to protect DVDs and video games doesn't necessarily mean the founding fathers were dead set against it.

This was the constitutional issue that came before the United States Supreme Court in 1884 in a landmark case known as *Burrow-Giles Lithographic Co. v. Sarony*. Napoleon Sarony was a photographer who had taken a posed portrait photo of the famed writer Oscar Wilde. Without attaining permission, Burrow-Giles Lithographic Co. made copies of the photo for sale to the public. Mr. Sarony sued alleging that the lithographic company's appropriation of the image violated his copyright in the photograph. The company's defense was that photography was not a *writing* of an *author*, and, as such, it was not entitled to copyright protection. The defendant corporation further argued that a photograph is simply a mechanical reproduction of the exact features of some object, and that recording those features with a camera doesn't constitute authorship.

The Supreme Court disagreed with that argument. Associate Justice Samuel Freeman Miller composed the Court's published ruling. In it he wrote, "We entertain no doubt that the Constitution is broad enough to cover an act authorizing copyright of photographs, so far as they are representatives of original intellectual conceptions of the author." Addressing the question of whether the photograph did indeed represent original intellectual conceptions, the Court rationalized that the photographer had exercised acts of authorship by doing such things as posing his subject, selecting and arranging wardrobe and other accessories, arranging the lighting, and evoking the desired expression. As such, the photograph was deemed protectable by copyright. That ruling, which stands as good law to this day, opened the door for Congress to extend copyright protection to creative works of many varieties and media.

However, there are some works of authorship that are specifically prohibited from being copyrighted. The same section of the Copyright Act that defines what constitutes a work of authorship also spells out what does *not* qualify for copyright protection. The statute reads:

> *In no case does copyright protection for an original work of authorship extend to any idea, procedure, process, system, method of operation, concept, principle, or discovery, regardless of the form in which it is described, explained, illustrated, or embodied in such work.*[3]

That means your brilliant idea for a movie, in which college cheerleaders buy a ship and become pirates on the high seas, isn't copyrightable. Nor is your stunning directorial concept to set *Romeo and Juliet* in a Las Vegas casino, or your dazzling method of playing the zither with your earlobe. While each of these might be a stroke of genius, none is a protectable piece of intellectual property under the Copyright Act. Additionally, note that the statutory language makes it clear that the prohibition applies even to thoroughly *original* works. You can't claim that you're entitled to copyright protection just because you're the first person ever to think up some great, unique, never-before-conceived-of idea. Originality, in this case, doesn't do a thing to supersede the restrictions. Should you write a book on the topic, you'd be entitled to copyright the wording you use to explain how to play the zither with an earlobe. But you couldn't copyright the *method* of earlobe zither playing, and someone else could come along later and write another book describing the exact same method (that is, so long as that second author uses different wording from that used in your book), and there would be no violation of copyright law.

---

3   17 U.S.C. § 102(b).

Names and titles are also not copyrightable. There's both a novel and a song titled *Gone with the Wind*, and there are two songs written in different eras that each have the title *For All We Know*. There's no copyright infringement in either example. Competing works with the same title might raise legal issues involving claims of *unfair competition* (something we'll get into in a later chapter), but not copyright claims. The same holds true for common graphic designs or other visual ornamentation. You can't copyright a fleur de lis or a yin-yang symbol. Federal regulations prohibit that sort of thing.[4] But you might be able to copyright an original design that incorporates those symbols.

Despite the Act's attempt to specify exactly what is and isn't included, there are still some gray areas when it comes to copyrightable subject matter. One such example would be musical arrangements. Ordinarily, the composer owns the copyright to an original song, and another person doing merely a stylized version of that song has never been viewed as creating a distinctly copyrightable derivative work. Courts that have dealt with such cases have basically said that a musical arrangement can't be a copyrightable work where it simply adds inconsequential embellishments that any competent musician might have improvised. However, in the 1993 case of *Tempo Music, Inc. v. Famous Music Corp.*, a federal court in New York City tried a legal battle between the estate of Duke Ellington and the estate of Billy Strayhorn over the intellectual property rights of Mr. Strayhorn's arrangement of Mr. Ellington's song, *Satin Doll*. Mr. Strayhorn's arrangement of the hit song was particularly notable for including certain famous harmonic elements, and the court noted that, while harmony is often limited by the underlying melody, it's not always just a byproduct of the melody. The court allowed that a certain amount of creativity goes into arrangements that influence "the mood, feel, and sound of a piece," and the court refused to rule that there could never be any circumstances under which the independently composed harmony of a song might be copyrightable. In another case, a different court ruled that even common guitar riffs in a song could be separately protected by copyright if they constitute something recognizably the artist's own and are not just a trivial variation. Of course, defining what amounts to

---

4   In the Code of Federal Regulations, 37 C.F.R. § 202.1(a) specifically states that "words and short phrases such as names, titles, and slogans; familiar symbols or designs; mere variations of typographic ornamentation, lettering or coloring" are examples of works not subject to copyright protection.

a *recognizable, non-trivial* variation is something that defies my ability to provide you with a bright-line rule suitable for every situation. Let's just say it's an arguably gray area.

Over the years, courts have wrestled with the question of whether literary characters can be copyrighted. As we said, names are not copyrightable. So, if you want to write a story about an accountant in Boston who just happens to be named Scarlett O'Hara, you won't be infringing a copyright using that character name. But what if you want to write a story about someone named Wonder Woman who possesses super powers? There you're likely to run into super trouble. Generally, similarities between characters are not automatic grounds for copyright infringement. If that were the case, there would probably be only one cops-and-robbers show on television, because the similarities between many of the characters on such shows sometimes make them almost indistinguishable from one another. The courts have been reluctant to rule that mere character similarities are an infringement, because the courts don't want to deter the creativity that copyright laws are meant to promote. However, they will look at the totality of a character's visual image, as well as its description and traits in determining whether those characteristics are of such a degree as to make the character, itself, copyrightable.

Superheroes are particularly notable for acquiring copyright protection. In these cases, the descriptions of what these characters look like, the outfits they wear, and the marvels they do are typically such that any similarly crafted character would almost immediately conjure the original character into the mind of the audience. Cartoon and comic strip characters are also especially suitable for copyright. Here the character's traits are not only identifiable but also the character's specific look. There's no mistaking Charlie Brown's appearance, and any attempt to create a similar character with a similar look would likely result in a copyright infringement action. But that doesn't mean one is prohibited from creating a character that has some of the same traits as Charlie Brown. One could argue that Woody Allen's neurotic nebbish character from his movies contains some of the same Charlie Brown-like traits. However, neither is infringing the other because neither, in its totality, is a duplication of the other character.

Another copyright issue—hotly contested between playwrights and theatrical directors—involves the stage directions that a director adds to a particular production of a stage play. Directors and their union (the Stage Directors and Choreographers Society) started making waves in the late 20th century when they began claiming that stage directions should be something that can be copyrighted independent of the copyright the author holds on the script. The argument the directors make is that their contribution to the performance of a play—that is, specific notations of actor movements, stage dressing, thematic elements, and the like, things that aren't specifically referenced in or inferred from the script—are the director's own intellectual property deserving of its own protection against copycats. (And, believe me, nothing gets a director more steamed than when he sees his ideas being swiped by some other director at another theater doing the same play.) Meanwhile, playwrights and their guild (the Dramatists Guild of America) have long maintained that the Copyright Act explicitly denies protection to "concepts" such as a director's interpretation of the look or feel of a drama, and that stage directions are merely an extension of what's called for in the script. Additionally, playwrights argue that, to allow a director to lock up certain movements, settings, or moods related to production, would be to allow that director to prohibit the use of those movements, settings, or moods in future performances of the play, and such control, playwrights contend, is legally reserved exclusively to the play's copyright holder—namely, the playwright. Like the question related to musical arrangements, it's a highly debatable issue that keeps popping up over and over.[5]

Copyright protection can also get a little hazy where aesthetics and utility merge. An example of this could be a lamp that serves the utilitarian function of providing illumination but that also possesses in its structural form an original design of pictorial, graphic, or sculptural features. Think about a lamp that has a base shaped like a mermaid. One could debate the quality of the art but not the fact that a mermaid statuette—even in a lamp— is an artistic expression wholly separate from the illumination function of the lamp. The bulb doesn't need the mermaid for it to light, and the mermaid doesn't need the light bulb for it to be an artistic expression. As such, the statuette of the mermaid is copyrightable.

---

5   If you're really interested in the legal issues over whether stage directions could attain copyright protection (and almost every director and playwright I know is very interested in that), I wrote a much more detailed legal analysis that was published in the *Arizona Law Review* in 2001. It's titled *Elvis Karaoke Shakespeare and the Search for a Copyrightable Stage Direction.* (The official citation is 43 ARIZ. L. REV. 677.) You can access it online at the *Arizona Law Review's* online archives at www.law.arizona. edu/Journals/ALR/ALR2001/content_v43n3.cfm . You can also access that law review archive from my law office website at amadalaw.com/articles.htm.

With this knowledge, now ask yourself whether a belt buckle is eligible for copyright protection. Surely, the belt won't hold together without the buckle. So it would be impossible to say that the two could coexist separately, each as an independent article of apparel. However, while the buckle might be an indispensible component of the belt, the *shape and design* of the buckle is not absolutely dictated by functional necessity. Design a belt buckle that looks just like the face of your Aunt Rhoda, and, while the functional element of it can't be copyrighted, the artistic design can. The exception to this is where the design is necessitated by its function. An example would be a clothing store mannequin. The mannequin's form is dictated by the need for it to wear the clothing it's exhibiting to the store's customers. Therefore, whatever artistic expression is contained within its design is superseded by the utilitarian function it's meant to serve. To grant a copyright for such things would be to place a restraint on the manufacture and marketing of utilitarian products, and that's not the function of copyright. That's the function of patents. So, even if you've designed the mannequin's form to be an exact replica of Aunt Rhoda's unique body type, you can't copyright it.

Attaining, Using, and Keeping a Copyright

Now that you know what kinds of things can and can't be copyrighted—or, at least, have some guidelines to help you make that determination—let's talk a little about the process of attaining copyright.

As I stated earlier, copyright is automatically attained for all "original works of authorship fixed in any tangible medium of expression." The two key words we'll concentrate on here are "original" and "fixed." We'll start with "original."

Original, for the purposes of copyright, does *not* necessarily mean there's a requirement that you be the first person in the history of the world ever to come up with the idea for the work. It only requires that the work be the product of your own independent labor or genius. That somebody else previously came up with a very similar or even identical creative work doesn't mean you're not entitled to copyright what you've done. I know this sounds incredibly odd to most people. But the fact is, if you were to conceive of a novel about an Oklahoma family leaving the Dust Bowl of the Great Depression to seek migrant farm work in California, and even if you titled it *The Grapes of Wrath*, and even if every word in your book was identical to the book authored by John Steinbeck, you'd still be entitled to a copyright on your book so long as you can show that you had never encountered or heard of Mr. Steinbeck's book and that the similarities were purely coincidental. In this case, *original* isn't synonymous with *unique*. It simply means that the work was an original creation of yours rather than a copy you made of someone else's work. Similarities to works you've never heard of don't disqualify your original work from copyright protection. (Of course, if you write an identical copy of *The Grapes of Wrath* and claim it's your original work, you're going to have some explaining to do as to how you just happened to reproduce such a well-known work without having had any knowledge of it whatsoever. And good luck making that argument before the judge. Let me know how that works out.)

Once again, copyrights should not be confused with patents. Because patents protect against a competitor marketing a similar product that has only minor or cosmetic differences, the Patent and Trademark Office conducts a long, painstaking examination of all applications to ensure that the product truly is unique. Only once the Patent and Trademark Office is satisfied that the item before it is unlike any other already patented item will it grant the patent request. In contrast, the Copyright Office makes no such examination of the applications it receives. Because copyright laws make no requirement of uniqueness, there's no need for the Copyright Office to engage in a hunt for similar copyrighted works. So long as the application is made correctly and the work being submitted falls into one of the enumerated categories eligible for copyright, the Copyright Office will simply stamp the form and register the copyright. Should there later be claims that one registered work infringes another, that's a matter for the courts and not the Copyright Office to decide.

Turning to the other key word—*fixed*—it's terribly important to remember that, despite the often intangible nature of intellectual property, copyright protection doesn't attach to a work unless it's fixed in some tangible medium of expression. It doesn't matter what that medium is—a writing, a recording, an illustration, etc. It only matters that it be set in some format that can then be shared with others. Lacking that fixation, there's no copyright protection.

Performing artists are particularly susceptible to giving away what could be copyrightable material if they're accustomed to doing performances "on the fly" without a prepared script. Like any other artistic creation, a performance has no copyright protection unless it's recorded in some format capable of being replayed or recreated at a later time. For example, if you sit down at a piano and start making up a tune on the keyboard, and you haven't written out the notes of the music or previously made an audio recording of the song, that's music that's free for the taking by anyone who comes along and happens to hear it. It's music that hasn't been fixed in a tangible format.

Now before you get too carried away with the notion that you're going to start audio or video recording every creative move you ever make in order to claim a copyright on it, it should be noted that just because you make a video recording of yourself playing Blanche DuBois in *A Streetcar Named Desire* doesn't mean that every other actress who subsequently plays the role will now have to pay you a royalty. You didn't create, and you don't own the underlying drama. At most, assuming you're the one who made the video, you own the copyright on that video. What's more, before you go making videos of copyright protected plays, you'd better get permission from the copyright holder. Otherwise you could be charged with making an unauthorized copy of a play that was, itself, fixed in a tangible medium of expression—namely, the script.

While we're on the subject, let's focus on what exactly a copyright is.

Break the word down into its two root word components: *copy* and *right*. Possessing a copyright is possessing the *right* to make a *copy*. This is the very foundation of copyright law. You can buy a painting from a gallery and take that painting home with you, or you could turn around and give or sell the painting to someone else. But, unless you've specifically also purchased the copyright to that work of art, you cannot make an exact copy of it and give away or sell that copy on the open market. That right to make a copy is a right you don't possess. It's a right that belongs exclusively to the artist until such time as the artist explicitly gives that right to someone else.

Unauthorized copying happens ubiquitously in the world of recorded music. You buy a music recording, and you decide your best friend should also hear this. So you make a copy and give it to your friend. Although well-meaning, technically that's a violation of copyright law. You've made a copy of a copyright protected recording and distributed it to someone other than yourself. Now I know I probably don't need to spell this out for the music artists who are reading this, but, for the benefit of everyone else, think about it this way: When you gave your friend the copy, that's one less copy of the music the copyright holder gets to sell, because now your friend doesn't need to buy his own copy of the recording. That's exactly the kind of thing copyright laws attempt to prevent. By reserving to the artist the exclusive right to make copies of the art, the law preserves for that artist the ability to make a profit from that art. If anyone who came in contact with the art were allowed to copy it and distribute it on his own, the artist's ability to benefit financially from the marketing of his own art would be seriously curtailed, thus, reducing an artist's incentive to create. That would be a direct contradiction of the Constitution's language granting Congress the power "To promote the Progress of...useful Arts" through copyright laws.

While the law does spell out some very specific exceptions—most of which you'll probably never have any reason to worry about and some of which we'll cover later in this book—under Section 106 of the Copyright Act, a copyright owner possesses the *exclusive* right to make (or authorize someone else to make) a reproduction of the copyrighted work and to distribute the work through sale, rental, leasing, or lending. That exclusive right further extends to public performance or public display of the work. In the case of sound recordings, it also includes the right to publicly perform the work by means of digital audio transmission.

Additionally—and a highly notable addition it is—the copyright owner holds the exclusive right to prepare *derivative works* based on the copyrighted work. A motion picture adaptation of your book; a musical adaptation of your drama; a translation of your song lyrics; a sound recording of your poetry; a poster reproduction of your drawing; a T-shirt sporting your photograph; a computer game based on your comic strip—all are examples of derivative works. The artist does not necessarily have to create the derivative himself. He can authorize someone else to do it and, under our "bundle of sticks" property doctrine, allow that other person to create only such derivative works as the author approves, reserving the potential to create other derivative products for another time and place. Obviously, the marketing of derivative products can be a profitable venture for the artist who controls that privilege, and some have even done better for themselves by authorizing someone else's derivative of their work than they have with the marketing of their own original works. Lynn Riggs, for example, was a writer whose plays had a handful of short runs on Broadway, and he probably made a bit of money for himself when he was writing Sherlock Holmes screenplays for Hollywood. But at least some of his biographers suggest that his best and most reliable income only started rolling in after his play, *Green Grow the Lilacs*, was taken up by a couple of new collaborators who adapted it into a musical. Those collaborators were Richard Rodgers and Oscar Hammerstein II. They called the musical *Oklahoma!* And the rest, as they say, is history.

No discussion of copyright would be complete without turning to the question of *duration*. How long does a copyright last?

Initially, under the very first American copyright act, copyrights were granted for a term of fourteen years with the possibility of renewal for another fourteen years. Over time, Congress has stretched that out, and, as of this writing, a copyright under the current law lasts for the duration of the creator's life plus an additional seventy years. Renewals are no longer necessary or a part of the process. In cases where there's more than one creator involved in a joint effort, the copyright endures for the duration of the last surviving creator plus an additional seventy years. Where the work was made anonymously or under a pseudonym that hides the true identity of the creator, the copyright lasts for ninety-five years from the year of its first publication or 120 years from the year of its creation, whichever comes first. The 95/120 year limitation also applies to works created under a *work made for hire* arrangement. We'll talk more about those arrangements later.

For those who worry about the dangers of marketing one's work in this global economy in which we now live, you'll be happy to know that copyright protections for your work extend beyond the United States. By treaties, most of the world's nations abide by agreements to respect and allow for the enforcement of protections of another nation's citizen's copyrighted material within their borders. A detailed analysis of how copyright protections might work in different parts of the world under different circumstances is a subject on which I expect full treatises could likely be written, and it's well beyond the scope of what I'm going to attempt here. For now, just know that, if that sniveling little wiener who works down the hall from you thinks he's going to grab your five-year-old's finger painting off your wall when you're not looking and run it up to Canada to market reproductions of it as "folk art," he's not gonna get away with it.

Trademark Basics

At some point in an artist's career—perhaps at a time when the sales of his art start to result in good fortune shining down upon him economically—the artist may think to himself, "Gee, isn't there some law that protects my art's marketing from the ravages of copycats and wannabes who make confusingly similar works just to cash in on my fame and success?" Well, there is. It's the law of *trademark*.

Now I can hear some of you already. You're saying, "Trademarks? Those are for big corporations with big products and fancy ad campaigns that involve slick slogans. That's not what I'm about. I don't want to open up an office on Madison Avenue. I just want to sell my art."

That point notwithstanding, trademark law isn't reserved only for mega corporations with multi-million-dollar budgets. It can also be employed by small companies, and even solitary individuals, to distinguish and protect their marketing of products and services, even when those products and services aren't household names the world over.

If, for example, Joan is well known in her community as a professional clown entertainer who markets clown make-up, she could trademark the name of her business—let's just call it *Wingo the Clown Make-up*—so as to distinguish it from any other clowns in town offering similar products. The trademark would protect Joan from someone else coming along later and setting up a competing operation also called *Wingo the Clown Make-up*. A second company with the same name could confuse potential customers who, looking for the products of Wingo the Clown, might then mistakenly purchase the make-up of the latter day *Wingo* rather than Joan's product. It would be unfair for Joan to lose business to someone else, not because that other person's offering a superior product or service but simply because that other person is unjustifiably capitalizing on the goodwill Joan has acquired for her own business.

Confusion—or, more precisely, the *avoidance of confusion*—is at the very heart of trademark law. Unlike copyright, which is rooted in the idea of protecting the artist from infringers, the crux of trademark is based on the notion of protecting the consuming public from being deceived or misled. I know that sounds counterintuitive to many. When someone's accused of misusing someone else's trademark, it's not the consuming public that brings the lawsuit. It's the company whose trademark has been misappropriated that "lawyers up" and marches into battle to win it back. But the trademark laws are public-spirited in that they provide us with a means of identifying particular products and not mistaking them for something else. Unique trademarks give us a quick and easy means of locating what we want in a market flooded with options.

Imagine, for example, that one morning you're eating a breakfast cereal called Shredded Flax, and you say to yourself, "This is the best darned cereal I've ever tasted! I'm buying it again the next time I go to the store!" Now imagine that you live in a world without trademarks. The next time you're in the supermarket, you go looking for that same cereal made by the same company, but there are no distinctive words or images on the boxes to distinguish the cereal you liked from any of the other brands of shredded flax cereals on the shelves. The result is that you, the consumer, are left to guess which of the various brands of cereal is the one you actually want, and you just might guess wrong, leaving you to ponder one morning at the breakfast table, "Why did I think this crappy cereal was any good?" So trademarks are good for all of us.

There's no getting around the fact that trademark is a *business* rather than an *artistic* protection. You can't simply trademark your art because you don't like the idea of some other artist doing something similar. Trademarks are reserved exclusively for those things that are put into commerce. If you're a sculptor who makes wind chimes out of small, ceramic creations, you can't slap a trademark name or logo on those chimes and qualify them for trademark protection until you actually put them on the open market for sale. Remember, you have to be carrying on some type of *trade* to qualify for a trademark. Constructing wind chimes just for the amusement of your family and friends won't cut it.

Although we've been talking about commercial marketing and merchandising, it should be noted that nonprofits can qualify for trademarks, too. So long as the trademark applies to something that's being put into the stream of commerce, it doesn't matter that the company holding the trademark is a nonprofit entity.

Here are a few more—but absolutely not the only—examples of other artistic endeavors that might also be trademarked: the name of a band; the name of a theater company; the name of an art gallery; and the name of a recurring event (such as a periodic film festival, music festival, or the like). Characters, and particularly cartoon characters, sometimes also become trademarks of various pieces of merchandise. The character itself is not trademarked but rather *serves as the trademark*, affording it an extra protection that it wouldn't have if it were only protected by copyright.

Unlike copyright, trademarks are not automatic. They don't happen just because you start carrying on a trade. You've got to take one of two affirmative steps.

The first and simplest thing you can do is to affix the letters "TM" next to the words or logo that you're using as a trademark. You don't have to file anything to do this. You don't have to register anything. Simply placing the "TM" next to your trademark gives notice to those who come in contact with it that you're claiming common law trademark rights. This informal method of claiming a trademark is typically done either: (1) because the trademark doesn't qualify for official registration; or (2) because the operation of the business being conducted doesn't really extend beyond a small geographic area, and there's little chance it will come in contact with other similar marks in other parts of the world.

In addition to the "TM" symbol, there is also the "SM" symbol for *service marks*. The difference between a trademark and a service mark is that the latter applies specifically to a particular service being offered. To provide an example, let's go back to Joan and her trademarked clown make-up business, *Wingo the Clown Make-up*. Now let's suppose that, as part of that business, Joan also offers a special service in which she will paint a child's face with clown make-up in less than thirty seconds using a special technique she's devised. She calls the service *Face in a Flash*. That offering isn't a business by itself or a tangible product of its own but simply a service *Wingo the Clown Make-up* ™ provides. As such, Joan might designate it *Face in a Flash* SM to lay claim to that phrase as her own service mark. A service mark carries with it the same protections as a trademark.

The second and more formal act of claiming a trademark involves registering it either with the United States Patent and Trademark Office or with the appropriate agency of your state. Naturally, a state registration applies trademark protections only within that state, whereas a federal trademark registration applies protections nationwide. Once granted a federal registration, you get to replace the informal "TM" with the more formal symbol ® or the words "Registered U.S. Patent and Trademark Office" (or the abbreviated "Reg U.S. Pat. & Tm. Off.").[6]

To get a federal registration, you have to show either that you are actually using the mark in commerce or you have a *bona fide intention* of using the mark in commerce. What's meant by bona fide intention? Simply put, it just means you're going to need to show more than just an inclination that you "might give it a try someday." You're not allowed to register a mark just to hold it for possible future use. You have to be serious about actually using

---

6   For more information on federal registration of trademarks, you can visit the website of
     the U.S. Patent and Trademark Office at www.uspto.gov.

the mark, if not immediately, then in the very near future to help you sell whatever it is you're marketing.

There are some limits as to what one can use as a trademark. For example, generic terms or terms that are merely descriptive can't be trade-marked. Calling your dance studio *The Dance Studio,* and then trying to get a registered trademark on that name, just isn't going to fly. No one's allowed to trademark a descriptive term that people apply generally to all similar things (unless that term acquires a secondary meaning that is recognized by the general public as applying to one and only one source). It would under-mine the free trade system if only one person were allowed to call a dance studio a "dance studio."

One can actually lose an already established trademark if it falls into common usage as a generic term. Perhaps the most famous case of that hap-pening was *Bayer Co. v. United Drug Co.* Near the end of the 19th century, Bayer came out with a new wonder drug it called "Aspirin." That wasn't the drug's generic name. It was the name Bayer came up with to market it. However, the term fell into common use as a generic name rather than a brand name, and Bayer didn't adequately counter that. The result was that Bayer lost its trademark to the name, "Aspirin," and to this day it remains a generally acknowledged descriptive word that any drug company may put on the label of that type of product. Since then, companies have been more careful about guarding their trademarks from becoming generic terms. Xerox, for example, is a company whose trademark name might have turned into a generic term if it weren't for a concerted effort by the company to prevent that. Many people are accustomed to saying they're "going to Xerox a copy" of something when, in fact, what they mean is that they're going to photocopy it. The Xerox company remains ever vigilant in its battle to remind the world that "Xerox" is not a verb.

It's also possible to lose a federal trademark registration if you cease using the mark in commerce. What's more, a mark could be taken off the register or barred from registration altogether if it's deemed to be immoral, scandalous, or disparaging. (Keep that in mind when you're trying to come up with a really *edgy* name for your head-banger band.)

Marks that are deceptive or misleading are likewise prohibited from federal trademark registration. You can title your online photo store *Nantucket Seascapes Photomart,* but, if you aren't really located in Nantucket and the seascape photos are actually photos of the Jersey Shore, you could be accused of deliberately trying to deceive your customers into thinking they're buying photos of one place when you're really selling them photos of another place. It's not a question of whether one photo is better than another. I, myself, was born and raised in New Jersey, and I loved going to the Jersey Shore when I was a boy. Photos of the state's seaside bring back fond memories for me. However, that's beside the point. If I want or have some particular need of a photo of the coastline of Nantucket, it would be a disservice to me to be misled into buying a photo of someplace else. Such deceiving trademarks could be barred from federal registration.

You can still claim a common law trademark even if barred from the federal register, and, depending on your state's rules, you might also be able to register your trademark with the state despite any bars to registering it with the federal government.

The one thing you absolutely can't do, though, regardless of whether it's a common law or registered trademark, is use a trademark that's deceptively similar to one that's already in use. That would defeat the whole purpose of the trademark, and it's not allowed. Unlike copyrights, trademarks have a requirement that they be unique when compared to any other mark in the same or similar industry. If you file for registration with the Patent and Trademark Office, that office will conduct a search to ensure that what you're trying to trademark doesn't infringe on any other trademark in the nationwide registry. If you're opting for the common law "TM" trademark, it's up to you to make sure your mark isn't similar to another that's already being used in your marketing area.

You'll probably be able to get away with having a similar trademark to someone who's in an entirely different line of work. There's unlikely to be any confusion in the public's mind as to whether Lefty's Polka Band and Lefty's Auto Body Shop are one and the same. But Lefty's Polka Band might be confused with Lefty's Salsa Band, and that could prompt a cease and desist letter from the other Lefty's lawyer. On the other hand, even if there are two different bands that both go by the name of Lefty's Polka Band, if they operate in completely different parts of the country, there's much less chance that the public will be confused. Therefore, so long as they don't cross into each other's territory, there's probably no problem with each holding an identical trademark.

So what happens if someone's operating with a common law, regional trademark or a state registered trademark, and someone else comes along later and registers an identical trademark on the national register? Such things have been known to happen, and, where someone has been legally using a particular, localized trademark, a latter day registrant on the national register cannot force that earlier user to give up his existing mark. In such cases, the national registrant just needs to live with the idea that somewhere someone holds the legal right to use the exact same trademark. However, it should be noted that, once there's a national registration for the mark, the person who has only a common law or state registration for the same mark will not be allowed to extend the use of that mark outside of the region where he's currently using it. In essence, the national registration zones off all other parts of the country that haven't previously been infiltrated by the non-registered mark.

Speaking of geography, it's important to note that registered trademarks do not have the same protections automatically in other countries. If you're expecting the marketing of your work to have a more global scope, and you want your trademark to have registered protection outside the United States, then you need to register your mark in each country where you want that protection to exist. Yes, I know that sounds like an incredible amount of work, registering your trademark in each and every country on the planet. And I'm sure it is. But, in all honesty, do you really expect to be actively marketing your art in Latvia?...I mean, anytime soon?...Okay, that's what I thought. So, for most artists, this is probably a nonissue.

With all this talk about trademark and its protections, it's important to remember that trademark is not a substitute for copyright. Nor can it be used to get around copyright's limitations. For instance, you can't overcome your inability to copyright a title by trying to trademark it. Trust me, you're not the first to come up with a brainstorm that goes something like this:
"Hey, I've got a great idea to make sure no one else can use the title of my book."
"How's that?"
"I'm gonna trademark it!"
"Ummm...but aren't trademarks only for things that identify a market-able commodity?"
"Yeah, but I *am* marketing a commodity with the title."
"What's that?"
"The book!"

File this one under "Nice try, but... ." I assure you that nobody at the Patent and Trademark Office is going to slap his forehead in astonishment and stamp the trademark application approved while marveling that no one ever came up with this stroke of genius before. Trademark laws were not enacted to circumvent copyright laws. Attempts to get too cute with things like that are likely to meet with instant disapproval. If it's a questionable call, do what I always recommend you do when confronted with a legal issue about which you're uncertain—consult a lawyer.

A huge difference between trademark and copyright is that trademark has no set expiration date. So long as the trademark's consistently used in commerce, it can be maintained indefinitely. Companies can and do keep their trademarked names and logos for centuries, with no expectation that they'll be giving up those marks anytime in the foreseeable future. If you, as an artist, create a business involving your art, that business could continue with your trademarks intact long after you're gone and the business has passed to your heirs or has been sold to someone else. (You've probably noticed that some musical bands carry on the trademarked name of the band even after there aren't any of the original members left. The Sons of the Pioneers are probably more like the great-grandsons of the pioneers by now.) A trademark, like all the other sticks in the artist's bundle, is a property right, and it's a right that can go on and on. It can be exploited, sold, bequeathed, given away, or squandered.

What Is the Artist Selling?

Okay, now that we've got a basic foundation in artistic property rights—that is, now that we know what it is the artist actually owns when art is created—we can take the next big leap to the commercial marketing of that art. You've gone through all the trouble of making art that helps beautify, stimulate, provoke, enlighten, educate, and generally enrich this world in which we live. The very least the world can do is let you make a buck on it. So we turn now to the all-important subject of selling. I know there are many artists who find it distasteful to equate their work with a business. However, if you have ambitions of being a professional artist—someone who gets paid for doing what you do—or you simply want your art to have a life beyond your immediate sphere of family and friends, you need to treat this end of the process as a business and have some understanding of exactly what it is you're trading when you come to some arrangement to sell or share your art with someone else.

This is the part where property law begins to meld with contract law. You know what it is you want to sell, and now you want to be sure that the deal is properly made so that you're parting with only what you intend and not what you don't intend to give away. Here, then, would be a good time for us to get into the basics of contracts.

A Meeting of Minds

A contract is nothing more than an agreement between two or more people who desire something to happen. Depending on the complexity of the arrangement, it could be a handshake deal or a signed document of hundreds of pages. But it all boils down to an understanding that the people making the contract are doing so because they wish to enlist cooperation in achieving a mutually acceptable outcome. If you want your friend's Jackie

Robinson baseball card and she wants your Ted Williams card, you could offer to trade cards. If your friend accepts, the deal is struck and each of you gets what you want. In an ideal situation, every party to a contract understands exactly what is expected of him (the card he must trade away) and exactly what he can expect in return (the card he will get in exchange). In an earlier age, this was known as *a meeting of minds*. Where there are ambiguities that make the terms of the agreement unclear, and the parties don't have an understanding of exactly what's being agreed to, the contract is flawed and its legal power suffers.

In the mid 19th century, an English court heard the famous case of *Raffles v. Wichelhaus*, which involved just such a situation. In that case, Wichelhaus had agreed to purchase a quantity of cotton from Raffles within a certain period of time after the cotton arrived from Bombay aboard a ship named the *Peerless*. Unbeknownst to either Raffles or Wichelhaus, there were two separate ships, each named the *Peerless*, and each sailing from Bombay to Liverpool—one arriving in October and one in December. Wichelhaus thought the contract involved the earlier shipment, and Raffles thought it was the later. The result was that, when the latter shipment of cotton arrived and Raffles tried to sell it to his buyer, Wichelhaus refused it because it arrived too late. Raffles sued to try to get Wichelhaus to honor the contract. The court ruled that, because the two parties each thought they were bargaining for something different, and neither had reason to believe the other's meaning was not the same as his own, there was no meeting of minds between them and, thus, no enforceable contract existed.

Despite that ruling, one shouldn't rely too heavily on a "meeting of minds" defense when it comes to contemporary contract law. Courts are less likely to void a contract where there was no deliberate misrepresentation and one party just didn't do his homework properly before entering into the agreement. The moral of the story: Know what you're getting into before you make a contract.

Contract law, in all its many intricacies, can be terribly complex, and there's no way I could possibly do justice to a comprehensive explanation of it in these pages. Nor do I expect that the audience for this particular work of prose would have the patience to wade through it were it to start to resemble a law school textbook. So, for our purposes, I'm going to keep this very simple and stick to just the rudimentary elements of what forms a contractual relationship. Basically, there are two ways it can be done.

The first involves the elements of *offer*, *acceptance*, and *consideration*.

Jesse says to Colleen, "I'll trade you my Ted Williams card for your Jackie Robinson card." That's an *offer*. Jesse has offered to give up his Williams card to Colleen if she, in return, will give up her Robinson card to him.

Colleen now has two options. She can decline the offer, in which case there is no agreement between them, or she can accept it, thus, acquiescing to the terms of Jesse's offer. If she says, "That's a deal," that's *acceptance*, and we have two of the three components necessary to form a contract.

It should be noted that if, rather than accepting the terms as Jesse proposed them, instead Colleen suggested a counteroffer (e.g., "I'll make the trade only if you throw in your Roberto Clemente card, too."), that counteroffer counts as a rejection of Jesse's original offer, and now it's up to Jesse to decide whether to accept Colleen's counteroffer. If Jesse doesn't accept, there's still no deal.

Assuming that these two eventually negotiate a proposal that's offered by one of them and accepted by the other, there's still the last component of a legal contract to account for—the *consideration*. For the purposes of contract law, consideration is the bartered-for inducement that causes one to want to enter into the agreement. It could be the gain or benefit to one party, or the loss or detriment to the other, that is the very reason for the contract. "Hey, let me have a dollar," is not an offer for a contract. The person handing over the dollar (should he decide to do so) gets nothing in return for forking over the buck. Hence, there's no consideration for the person giving the dollar. Whereas, "Hey, let me have a dollar and I'll wash the dishes for you," does have a tangible benefit for the person from whom the dollar is sought. If he accepts the offer and gives over the dollar, he gets out of having to do a household chore. Meanwhile, the person who offered to do the dishes gets the benefit he wanted, namely, the dollar. Both exchanges—dollar versus dishwashing—could be judged sufficient inducement to the agreement to count as consideration. Therefore, having all three elements—offer, acceptance, and consideration—this arrangement could be viewed as a legal contract.

Another method of establishing a contractual relationship is through *reliance*.

Let's say Jesse has an old clunker auto that hasn't worked in years, and he says to Colleen, "If you can get it running, you can have it." To make use of Jesse's offer, Colleen has major repairs done to the car at great cost to her.

Once the car's in working order, though, Jesse changes his mind and withdraws his offer. This hardly seems fair to Colleen. Although Jesse received no consideration for his offer to let Colleen have the car, Colleen relied on his promise when she invested her own money into fixing the auto's engine. Based on her detrimental reliance on Jesse's offer, a court might require Jesse to honor his promise to Colleen, or it could order him to compensate her for the money she's out. It would be just as if they had entered into a formal contract.

Sale of the Whole vs. Sale of Specific Rights

Sometimes transactions are simple. You set up a lemonade stand on the sidewalk in front of your home, and you offer the lemonade to passersby at fifty cents a cup. If someone takes you up on the offer and gives you fifty cents, you hand that person a cup of lemonade, and the transaction is concluded. You made an offer, it was accepted, and you each got the consideration you wanted. At that point, there's absolutely nothing about the deal that remains unsettled. You pocket the money. The purchaser gets to consume the beverage—or, for that matter, do anything else the purchaser wants to do with it since it's the buyer's cup of lemonade now. You can't ask the buyer to purchase the lemonade but not drink it, or to drink it but not enjoy the taste of it, or to promise to drink only half of it and throw the rest away. Oh, you could *ask*, but nobody buys lemonade under those types of conditions. So, when you're selling lemonade, you have an implicit understanding as the seller that, once you've parted with the beverage, you have no further claim on it. That type of transaction is a *sale of the whole*. That is, every right that goes along with possessing a cup of lemonade—the right to drink, savor, share, dispose of, water the petunias with it, etc.—is transferred from the seller to the purchaser upon completion of the transaction. In the business world, that's as simple as they come.

The sale of art, or any type of intellectual property, is seldom that simple. The reason is that artists don't often mean to imply that a buyer is entitled to do anything and everything with the artist's creation, even though buyers often assume that they are indeed acquiring unlimited rights when they purchase a work. For example, suppose you're a painter, and you've just sold to a local gallery your masterpiece, a portrait you call the *Mona Leta*. The buyer takes it back to the gallery and, for fun, paints a mustache on the portrait. Did you really mean when you sold the painting that you were also selling the right to deface your work? I mean, c'mon!—that's your name painted in the corner of the *Mona Leta* now sporting a cheesy handlebar mustache. What will people who see the painting think? How will it reflect on you as an artist? Chances are you never counted on this when you sold the painting. Meanwhile, the buyer never thought for an instant that he wasn't entitled to do whatever he wanted with a painting he purchased. After all, he *bought* it, didn't he? Obviously, there was something less than a meeting of minds on this transaction.

Another example: What about the musician who buys the sheet music to your song in a music store and then starts performing the song publicly because he thinks he's entitled to do that by virtue of the fact that he now owns a copy of the sheet music? The truth is that ownership of sheet music doesn't automatically equate to ownership of public performance rights to the song. When you sold your composition to the music publishing company, did you also sell it the public performance rights to be passed along to any Tom, Dick, or Harry who picks up the sheet music in a store? Probably not.

Going back to our proverbial bundle of sticks discussed in the previous chapter, we know that the property rights to any work can be sold off in their entirety or in piecemeal. Rights can be granted or reserved either explicitly or implicitly, depending on the agreement or the contract language. An example of language that explicitly states which rights are being sold might be:

> *The Seller grants to the Buyer the right to perform the song in all commercial public performance venues in all states west of the Mississippi River, including the state of Minnesota, but not including the state of Louisiana or any state located east of the Mississippi River.*

In the above example, the language spells out not only the exact region in which the right to perform the song is granted but also the region in which it's not granted. In the example, the seller has explicitly withheld the right of the buyer to perform the song east of the Mississippi. In the case of the two states that straddle both sides of the river, the contract has again given explicit instructions as to which state is included and which is excluded from the performance rights being granted. The same clause could have been written like this:

> *The Seller grants to the Buyer the right to perform the song in all commercial public performance venues in all states located*

in their entirety west of the Mississippi River, and also includ-
ing the state of Minnesota.

The second example means exactly the same as the first example, and it again spells out explicitly which region is included in the grant of performance rights. However, the performance rights to the excluded region are withheld *implicitly* by that region's absence from the description of the granted region. Obviously, if rights are granted only for Minnesota and all of the other states located entirely west of the Mississippi, the rights don't extend to any other state.

Note also in our example the phrase, "all commercial public performance venues." Such a phrase is a bit ambiguous for contract language. Exactly what does the seller mean by a "commercial public performance venue"? In many such cases, the agreement will attempt to define what's meant to avoid possible confusion later on. Again, the language could be explicit or implicit.

For the purposes of this Agreement, "commercial public perfor-
mance venues" is defined as and limited to concert halls, audi-
toriums, amphitheaters, bars, saloons, taverns, restaurants, and
cafes where admission is charged or where food and/or bever-
ages are served for a fee.

This wording defines and limits *explicitly* which venues are included in the performance rights grant. Shopping malls are not mentioned and so would be *implicitly* reserved by the seller as a venue where the performance rights are not conveyed to the buyer.

So long as we're talking about explicit contract language, it's important to note that many a contract dispute has erupted over the use of the word "include" or any of its derivative forms. Battles have raged over sentences such as:

The definition of the term "color" includes red, orange, yellow,
green, blue, indigo, and violet.

Does that sentence mean that the term "color" includes the specifically named colors as *examples* of what is intended by the clause, or is the term's definition limited to *only* those specifically named colors? Does pink qualify as a color if it's not explicitly named in the agreement? Or does it qualify because pink wasn't specifically excluded from the list of example colors? Courts may differ over how contract wording is to be interpreted, so you can see how important it is to word your agreements to say exactly what you mean. You probably don't want to leave it up to the courts to figure it out for you later on.[7]

...And now for something completely different...It's *Monty Python's Flying Circus* and a case that illustrates what we're talking about when we discuss the complexities of the contractual conveyance of intellectual property rights. Specifically, it's the case of *Gilliam v. American Broadcasting Companies.* This interesting case originally stemmed from the agreement the *Monty Python* creators had with the British Broadcasting Corporation when they produced their popular sketch comedy show for BBC television. The Pythons produced. The BBC broadcast. It was a successful relationship, and the program flourished. In fact, the show did so well that it attracted the attention of American television. PBS arranged to broadcast *Monty Python* on its network of public TV stations, and that's where many Americans got their first taste of *Python* humor.

Then, in 1973, Time-Life Films acquired the rights to the American distribution of some of the BBC's TV programs, among them *Monty Python*, and a deal was struck for ABC to broadcast some of the *Python* shows on the ABC television network. Among the big differences between PBS broadcasting and ABC broadcasting is the fact that the former is commercial free while the latter makes its money by inserting commercial advertisements periodically. The BBC is also a commercial free network, deriving its funding from the government. So, the BBC and PBS had virtually identical broadcast slots in terms of program time allotments. A half-hour time slot on either the BBC or PBS is actually about a twenty-eight-minute slot for the featured program. The same time slot on an American commercial network like ABC is one that actually affords only about twenty-two minutes to the featured program. The other eight minutes are dedicated to the

---

7   Drafting a contract can a very complex thing, loaded with all sorts of hidden pitfalls. The examples of contract language given in this book are in no way meant to be extracted and used verbatim to form specific agreements between parties. They are, at best, simple illustrations of possible clauses that represent what is being discussed in the text. If you're engaging in a formal business relationship, and you're not knowledgeable about the drafting of contracts for such things, I strongly urge you to consult a lawyer. It's always better to deal with lawyers while you're putting the project together than it is to deal with them while you're in court fighting over the deal that got loused up.

commercials. As a result, ABC couldn't shoehorn the twenty-eight minute *Monty Python* shows into its twenty-two minute time slots without some serious editing.[8] ABC took the scissors, so to speak, to the programs and chopped them down to size. When the Pythons saw what was done to their show in the editing room, they were appalled by what they viewed as the discontinuity and "mutilation" of the end product of their work. They filed suit against ABC, and the case made its way to the United States Court of Appeals for the Second Circuit.

In its ruling, the court acknowledged that the Pythons had granted the BBC broadcasting rights for their program, and those rights could legally be transferred to a third party such as ABC. However, the BBC was not free to sell what it didn't possess. Part of the agreement between the Pythons and the BBC stated that, while the BBC had the final authority to make changes to the broadcast programs, the Pythons had explicitly retained all rights to the underlying scripts. No major changes to the scripts could be made without prior consultation with the Pythons. The broadcast programs, as re-edited by ABC, constituted derivative works of the scripts, and the Pythons hadn't given their blessing to these derivative works. Because the Pythons hadn't sold the BBC the right to do this to the shows, the BBC didn't own that right. It was, to use our ubiquitous metaphor, a stick that the Pythons never gave up. As a result, while it had legally purchased the broadcasting rights from the BBC, ABC didn't—and couldn't—purchase a right to do the editing it had done. Such a right was not the BBC's to sell. The court ruled in the Pythons' favor, holding that ABC had committed copyright infringement by creating a derivative product it wasn't authorized to make.

---

8 It doesn't escape my notice that the uncut *Monty Python* shows also contain some racy material that didn't conform to American broadcasting standards of the 1970s. As such, it's unlikely that ABC could have gotten away with running the sketches that featured nudity or off-color language, and such material would have had to have been purged from any broadcast on ABC, lest it rouse the ire of conservative viewers, cautious advertisers, or the Federal Communications Commission.

It also doesn't escape my notice that these racy parts (which the Pythons, in their own lexicon, might refer to as the "naughty bits") were broadcast without censorship on PBS stations, apparently without creating an upheaval of protest or bringing down the wrath of the FCC with charges that such things were corrupting the minds of our nation's youth. I can only guess that this may have something to do with the fact that PBS stations used to bill themselves as "educational television," and perhaps our government just figured nobody under the age of eighteen would willingly go anywhere near anything that claimed to be "educational." Or maybe nobody in our government ever went anywhere near anything claiming to be "educational." As I said, it's only a guess.

So what do we learn from this case? We learn that, when dealing with the transfer of intellectual property from one person to another, you need to know exactly what you're selling or buying. It's easy when it's a cup of lemonade that has basically only one marketable end use; not so easy when you're transacting a product that could take on multiple forms in its marketing.

The privilege of exploiting and marketing forms of a work that are beyond the originally intended purpose is sometimes referred to as *subsidiary rights*, and these are often hotly negotiated matters in intellectual property deals. Think about the kind of money that must be involved in the sale of toy action figures based on the characters in a popular film or TV show. Wouldn't you like it if you were to get a dime for every *Transformers* ™ toy that's sold around the world? Well, so would everyone else. That's why the subsidiary rights (or *secondary rights*, as they're sometimes called) to a piece of intellectual property can be just as important—or sometimes even more important—as are the rights to the property's originally conceived purpose (or its *primary rights*). Naturally, when transacting business, everyone attempts to get the best deal possible, and you can't fault the buyers of your art for wanting the same. But you don't want to bargain away more than you intended or more than is fair to you. You're also entitled to get the best deal you're able to negotiate. So the word of caution here is to be especially careful about subsidiary rights to your work. If you're not careful, you could be trading away a possible fortune without realizing it until it's too late.

To give but a few examples—and in no way an exhaustive list—of potential subsidiary rights to intellectual property, such rights might include motion picture or television adaptation rights, audiovisual rights, dramatic or performance rights, and merchandising rights. A hugely lucrative market now also exists for the electronic rights to intellectual property. Computer games and other applications that are derivatives of a person's creative work have expanded the scope of subsidiary rights, and companies that purchase an artist's work now often include clauses in their contracts that explicitly guarantee the company a piece of any electronic derivatives or, for that matter, a piece of any derivatives created by or for *future technologies not now known*. The "future technologies" reference has become a standard part of such contracts. (Believe me, none of those companies wants to be left out in the cold should someone invent "smell-o-vision" a few years down the road.)

If you're an up-and-coming artist with little negotiating power, you might have to settle for dealing away all or most of the subsidiary rights to a creative work just so you can get your foot in the door. You might even have to sell your work as a whole, with all the rights bundled into one, that gives the buyer total control. If that's the only way you can make the sale, then that's the only way you can make the sale. That's business. That's life. Move on.

However, if there's only one clause that you, the artist, can negotiate into a contract for the sale of your work, that clause ought to be one that says something like:

> *All rights in the work not expressly granted by the Seller to the Buyer under this Agreement are wholly and exclusively reserved to the Seller.*

It's simply a catch-all clause that might be helpful should there later be a dispute over what was actually transferred in the sale. If you didn't mean for a right to be transferred, and that right wasn't explicitly transferred by the language in the contract, a clause such as the above could be used as evidence that you never gave up that right.

The one thing you never turn over by accident is the copyright to your work. Copyright ownership can be transferred only by a written instrument signed by the copyright owner or that owner's authorized agent.[9] That written transfer doesn't have to be its own separate document. It could be included as a clause in a larger contract. However, if the copyright is meant to be transferred as part of the agreement, the clause referencing that transfer must be in the contract somewhere. For clarity's sake, if you absolutely do *not* mean to transfer the copyright, it's probably in your best interest to insist that there be a clause in the contract stating that you reserve the copyright to yourself.

There are times when transferring your copyright to someone else is appropriate and acceptable. For example, a book publisher will typically require that the copyright be turned over to the publishing company so that it can print and market the book. However, the transfer of a copyright doesn't

---

9   The statutes governing this are 17 U.S.C. § 202 (stating that the mere possession of a work does not automatically transfer the underlying copyright embodied in that work) and 17 U.S.C. § 204 (requiring a signed writing to transfer ownership of a copyright).

necessarily mean the artist must part with that copyright for all time. It's possible to build into the contract clauses that limit the amount of time that a copyright is transferred; or the contract language could specify certain conditions under which the copyright reverts back to the artist. (E.g., a clause stating that, should the publisher not publish the book within twelve months of approval of the final draft, the copyright will revert to the author.) What's more, even if there isn't a contract clause explicitly permitting for copyright reversion, there's a provision of copyright law that allows for the artist or his heirs to terminate the transfer of the copyright after thirty-five or forty years.[10] There's a five-year window in which the termination can be effected by serving notice in writing to the then current copyright holder. That termination can be effected notwithstanding any agreement to the contrary. Even a so-called iron-clad contract signed in blood can't supersede federal law.

Licensing

Transactions involving intellectual property do not necessarily have to be outright sales. An alternative to selling your art is *licensing* it. Just like the selling of a work, the licensing of it can be broken down into very particular rights that are licensed or not licensed to the buyer (or *licensee*, if you prefer). In essence, an artist can allow someone some of the privileges of ownership without ever giving up ownership himself. It's sort of like renting out an apartment. Your tenant pays the rent and that tenant is entitled to live in the apartment, furnish it, decorate it, keep his possessions there, receive his mail there, and invite his friends in to visit. But he never actually owns the dwelling. Ownership remains firmly with the landlord. If the tenant doesn't pay the rent or violates any of the landlord's rules, the landlord can evict the tenant. The licensing of intellectual property works the same way.

A license is a temporary and revocable authorization of specific rights by the owner, and licenses are used all the time in the arts and entertainment fields. For example, the ticket that you buy for a seat at a performance or a

---

10   This provision is found in 17 U.S.C. § 203 (describing the means for the termination of transfers and licenses granted by the artist). In determining whether one has to wait thirty-five or forty years before termination can be effected, Section 203(a)(3) states:

> Termination of the grant may be effected at any time during a period of five years beginning at the end of thirty-five years from the date of execution of the grant; or, if the grant covers the right of publication of the work, the period begins at the end of thirty-five years from the date of publication of the work under the grant or at the end of forty years from the date of execution of the grant, whichever term ends earlier.

sporting event is a license. The person selling the ticket isn't actually selling you the chair you'll be sitting in. He's only selling you temporary permission to sit in that chair at a specific date and time while the event you paid to see is taking place. If the performance gets canceled or the ballgame gets rained out, the person who sold you the ticket simply revokes the license and either refunds your money or gives you a rain check.

Another common example of the licensing of a creative work is the granting of performance rights for a song. With few exceptions, a music artist doesn't purchase the actual song but, rather, just the permission to record or perform the song in public. The songwriter still holds all the rights of ownership to the music, including the copyright with all its inherent rights. Absolutely none of those is transferred to the music artist simply because that artist has been licensed to perform the song.

Yet another example of routinely licensed intellectual property is a dramatic performance. When a theater company contracts with a playwright or the playwright's publisher to attain the performance rights to a drama, what the theater company is buying is a dramatic performance license. Because the playwright hopes to see the play performed at more than one theater, he's unwilling to sell the play outright to one theater company. Instead, he licenses a company to do a public production of the play, reserving to himself the right to issue as many other performance licenses to other companies as he's able to arrange. (Note that simply buying a copy or copies of the script doesn't authorize one to produce the play. It's possible to *own* copies of the play but not be *licensed* to perform the play. These are two very distinct property rights and should not be confused with one another.) Because a license is revocable, dramatic performance licenses are sometimes issued and then later revoked by the copyright holder. Sometimes this is because of a breach of contract issue, and sometimes it's just because a larger theater company in the same geographic region desires the license. Because production companies don't want to compete against the same play in their area, dramatic performance licenses often contain a clause that assures the licensee there will be no other dramatic performance licenses issued for that play within a certain number of miles. That being the case, if a bigger theater company with more money to spend comes along wanting the rights to a play that a smaller company's already licensed to do in that same area, the playwright might just yank the license out from the smaller company and give it to the bigger one. I know that sounds pretty cold, but, as they say… it's a rough business, babe.

Even the purchase of a simple stencil template can involve a license of specific rights rather than an outright sale of the whole. The designer of the stencil holds the copyright on that particular pattern, and all that designer is selling you when you purchase the stencil template is the license to transfer that pattern to the surface of your choice by dabbing paint or some other coloring substance into the template's holes. The pattern still belongs to the person who created it, and, if you're not the copyright holder, you're not permitted to create a duplicate stencil pattern on your own template. If that were allowed, you'd be able to market a competing stencil product that would infringe on the original designer's copyright, and that's not part of the license you were given when you purchased the stencil.

Just in case I haven't been absolutely clear on this point, a license doesn't grant the licensee the right to do *whatever he wants* with the licensed intellectual property. The licensee's privileges extend only so far as the license specifically permits. For example, a theater company licensed to produce a play is not automatically authorized to revise the script or make additions or deletions to it. That would constitute the creation of a derivative work, and, without the authorization of the copyright holder, that's a violation of copyright law. Also, a musician who's licensed to perform a song at a live performance venue is not automatically authorized to make an audiovisual recording of that performance for later broadcast on television. Again, absent permission, that's a copyright violation. And a dancer who's licensed to perform someone else's choreography at a public concert is not allowed to represent to the public that the dance was his own choreography. That misrepresentation would violate federal law under the Lanham Act.[11] As always, licensing transfers only those rights specified by the license and nothing more.

The Artist as an Independent Contractor

It's always good to know where one stands in this world; and it's never more important to an artist than when you're doing a job for someone else. As an artist, you might get a contract to create a work of art—perhaps the commission you've always dreamed of that will finally allow you to produce your masterpiece. If you're a professional artist, or your goal is to

---

11   There will be more about the Lanham Act when we get into protections against unfair competition in the chapter titled "How Does the Artist Protect Intellectual Property?".

become one, then this sort of thing is probably among your grandest desires. However, your business relationship with a hiring party makes a big difference when determining the rights to the work you create. So you need to be aware of exactly what that relationship is when you take on a job to create art or any form of intellectual property.

There are two ways by which a person gets paid for the labor he performs. One way is as an *employee* of another person who contracts to provide that employee a set amount of compensation in return for the employee undertaking certain work projects dictated by the boss. Sound familiar? Sure. It's the way most of the world earns a living.

The second method by which labor is exchanged for money is one in which the person doing the labor is considered to be an *independent contractor*. An independent contractor is different from an employee in some key respects. In terms of the way the work is done, an independent contractor doesn't typically show up at the job site and do whatever work is assigned by the boss but, rather, contracts with the hiring party to do a specific task. Many, if not most artists fall into this latter category by virtue of the nature of the work artists do.

To illustrate this, let's devise a scenario of an independent contractor artist. We'll say that a sculptor named Andy has been selected by the BigBucks Corporation to create a sculptural work of art to grace BigBucks' corporate headquarters lobby. Andy doesn't work for BigBucks in any other capacity, and he has no office space or any other regular worksite at BigBucks. His usual place of work is his own studio. That's where he'll be crafting the artistic creation that will be installed in BigBucks' lobby. We'll assume that BigBucks' executives aren't sculptors, and they didn't design the sculpture that's being made. They simply selected it based on a design conceived and presented by Andy in response to the corporation's call for proposals. We'll further assume that, because the corporate execs aren't artists, and they have other matters concerning their own jobs to attend to, that they won't be supervising the daily progress or giving ongoing instruction to Andy as to the particulars of how to sculpt the artwork.

Andy's situation is a classic example of an independent contractor. He has been hired by BigBucks to create a work of art, but he hasn't been hired as an employee of the corporation. For the purposes of this type of venture, it would be no different than if Andy had a store in which he sold his works of art, and BigBucks simply selected one off the shelf. An artist doesn't become your employee just because you buy one of his works any more than a barber becomes your employee when you get a haircut. The artist, like the barber, retains an independence that's readily distinguishable from someone whose workday is fully controlled by his employer.

This is an important distinction because, in the absence of a contradictory agreement, an independent contractor retains all intellectual property rights to his art even after it has been sold and delivered to the buyer. Under the circumstances described above, Andy, as the creator of the sculpture, is the copyright holder, and, as we know, copyright isn't transferred unless there's a signed writing specifically stating that copyright ownership is being transferred. Andy can install the finished product at BigBucks, and, even if he never again goes anywhere near the corporation's headquarters, he still controls the right to make reproductions, create derivative works, or demand proper attribution as the work's creator wherever the work is displayed.[12]

The Work Made for Hire Doctrine

Now compare the above scenario to this one...

Let's say that Ed works as a designer in BigBuck's Advertising and Design Department. One day, Ed's supervisor comes to his desk and tells Ed that the big brass would like a new corporate logo, and the supervisor wants Ed to put aside whatever he's working on to design that logo. The supervisor might or might not give Ed guidance as to what type of logo to design. In this case it doesn't matter because, even if the creative genius is entirely Ed's brainchild, he's creating the art not of his own initiative on his own time but as part of his employment with BigBucks. What you create for your employer as part of your job duties is the property of your employer, and, as such, all intellectual property rights, including the copyright, automatically belong to the employer.

That doesn't mean that Ed can't punch out at the end of the workday, go home, design a creative work, and own all the intellectual property rights associated with original works of art. He absolutely can because, in this latter scenario, he's doing the creating for himself on his own time. His employer doesn't enter the equation on that one. But, when what you create is part of your regular job, that creation instantly becomes the property of the employer. This falls under the *work made for hire* doctrine as defined by Section 101 of the Copyright Act.

It's hard to dispute the logic of this. After all, if a person creates something specifically as a part of his employment, that employment is

---

12 Actually, proper attribution isn't a copyright matter but, rather, a federal protection under the Lanham Act. See p. 116.

convincingly argued to be the very reason the creative work was born. If you're a writer who works for a periodical that has you on staff and regularly assigns the writing projects that keep you gainfully employed, naturally that publication is going to be looked upon as the owner of the writings you produce for it, since those writing assignments wouldn't have occurred were it not for your employment with the periodical. What's more, it just makes sense from a practical standpoint that an employer often must own the rights to intellectual property that's fashioned specifically for it. If a television production company, for example, hires you as an animator for its weekly cartoon TV program, you can't expect that company to have to renegotiate with you every week for the intellectual property rights to the way you drew the characters in the previous show. Obviously, the company has to control the rights to the essential elements of the show it's producing, and it couldn't operate efficiently if those rights were under the power of various staff members, each of whom might put the kibosh on a particular production if that staff member's demands weren't met.

However, even if you aren't a regular staffer of the person hiring you, there are still situations where you, as an independent contractor, could create a work made for hire that would then belong to that employer. Again Section 101 of the Copyright Act states that a work made for hire is created when there's a signed, express agreement to that effect and the work being created is:

> *a work specially ordered or commissioned for use as a contribution to a collective work, as a part of a motion picture or other audiovisual work, as a translation, as a supplementary work, as a compilation, as an instructional text, as a test, as answer material for a test, or as an atlas... .*[13]

---

13 The Act defines "supplementary work" as "a work prepared for publication as a secondary adjunct to a work by another author for the purpose of introducing, concluding, illustrating, explaining, revising, commenting upon, or assisting in the use of the other work, such as forewords, afterwords, pictorial illustrations, maps, charts, tables, editorial notes, musical arrangements, answer material for tests, bibliographies, appendixes, and indexes... ." The Act further defines "instructional text" as "a literary, pictorial, or graphic work prepared for publication and with the purpose of use in systematic instructional activities." In 1999 *sound recordings* were also added to the list of commissioned works that could be considered a work made for hire. That addition lasted only a brief period of time, and it has since been removed. However, it illustrates the fact that laws can change, and you can't always rely on what was published at a given moment to be the most current information available about a law. That's why, when you're uncertain about the legal status of a particular issue, it's always wise to review the most current law or consult with an attorney who can advise you.

Often, contracts for the commission of such things will include the specific phrase, *work made for hire*, or sometimes just *work for hire*. Both phrases mean the same thing. If you sign a contract to create a work made for hire (or a work for hire) you're selling the work—as the saying goes—lock, stock, and barrel. When an artist contracts to create a work made for hire, that artist is agreeing to relinquish immediately any and all claims he might otherwise make on the work. That's not simply the physical possession of the work but, also, the copyright. Under this type of agreement, no signed, written transfer of the copyright is required, because technically, the moment the work is created, the copyright automatically belongs to the employer or purchaser. Therefore, since the artist never actually owns the copyright, no transfer of it is necessary.

Sometimes, even if the specific phrase is absent, one should still be careful about the nature of the work the artist is doing so as not to create a work made for hire unintentionally. In 1989, the Supreme Court of the United States dealt with this issue in the case of *Community for Creative Non-Violence v. Reid*. It was a case in which an artist was commissioned by an organization to produce a sculpture for it. This was your basic handshake agreement, and there was no written contract between the parties. So, when a dispute erupted over copyright ownership, the Court had to determine the nature of the arrangement on the circumstantial evidence derived from the facts of the case. At the heart of the matter was whether the sculptor, within the context of the work he did, could be considered an employee of the commissioning organization. The Court spelled out certain factors it took into consideration when determining whether a person is an "employee" of another. Those factors were:

- The hiring party's right to control the manner and means in which the work is created
- The skill required of the person hired for the task
- The source of the tools or other instrumentalities needed for the work
- The location where the work is done
- The length of time the hiring and hired parties have been associated professionally
- Whether the hiring party has the right to assign other tasks to the person being hired

- The extent to which the hiring party has discretion over when the work is done and for how long
- The method of payment
- The hired party's role in hiring or paying other people as assistants
- Whether the work being done is the type that could be considered a part of the hiring party's regular business
- Whether, in fact, the hiring party is in business
- Whether there are provisions for employee benefits involved
- The tax treatment of the person who was hired.

While acknowledging that the organization had directed the sculptor to the degree necessary to ensure that his final product would be what the organization wanted, the Court ruled in favor of the artist, saying he could not be considered an employee in this situation because the artist:

- Worked in a particularly skilled occupation as a sculptor
- Supplied his own tools
- Worked in his own studio
- Was retained by the organization for less than two months
- Could not be assigned additional projects by the organization, which had no right to make such additional assignments
- Was free to decide for himself when and for how long he worked
- Was paid his total compensation upon the completion of the project (something the Court noted was typical of the method by which independent contractors are paid)
- Had total discretion to hire his own assistants

Additionally, the Court noted that the creation of sculptures wasn't the organization's regular business, and, for that matter, the organization was a committee and not really a *business* at all, thus, meaning it wasn't an entity that typically hired employees. To cap it off, the Court also noted that the organization didn't pay payroll or social security taxes, didn't make contributions to unemployment insurance or workers' compensation funds, and didn't provide employee benefits. As such, in this particular case, it was a slam dunk win for the artist. He wasn't considered an employee of the commissioning organization. His sculpture wasn't a work made for hire.

Now this may sound like a resounding victory for artists over the work made for hire doctrine, but be forewarned that the Court also said that the organization might still have had a claim on the copyright of the work as a *joint author* because the organization's representatives had played such an integral role in the designing of what eventually became the final product. That could be a huge issue. But we'll get to a discussion of joint authorship when we talk about contractual relationships in a later chapter.

The Business Form

In the business world, a professional artist—that is, one who is actually selling art—needs to select a *business form*. Now, I'm not talking about one of those pre-printed papers with the little blank spaces that you fill in. I'm talking about the formal organization of your business as an artist. There are a few different options, and, while we're talking about business, let's take a quick look at what they are.

First, there is the option known as *sole proprietorship*. This is probably, by far, the most common business form adopted by independent artists. It requires no formal organization documents or filings. If you're setting up shop somewhere to sell your wares retail, you might need a business license or permit from the city or county, and, if you hire employees, you'll need to do the employer paperwork required by the Internal Revenue Service. (As a sole proprietor, you're also required to make quarterly estimated tax payments to the IRS and to the state, if your state also has an income tax.) But that's about it. If you decide to discontinue the operation, you can either sell all the assets to someone else or just stop conducting business. It's as simple as it gets—hence, its popularity as a business form.

The second option is a *partnership*, which can be formed between two or more people who carry on as business owners for profit. Like the sole proprietorship, no formal documents need be filed. However, to avoid misunderstandings that can quickly dissolve a partnership, it's usually best to draw up a partnership agreement that spells out how the arrangement will work. Absent an agreement that states otherwise, all partners have an equal vote in all decisions. Additionally, unless there's an agreement to the contrary, all profits are shared equally among the partners, regardless of who put up the most money or who has done the most work. Like the sole proprietorship, partners must make quarterly estimated tax payments and pay their own income taxes, but the partnership must also file an information tax report. A partnership is terminated if one partner withdraws or dies, and, unless the partnership agreement provides otherwise, a partnership interest can't be transferred to someone else. Partnerships that are formed with the intention that they exist only for a limited time and limited purpose are called *joint ventures*. Although joint ventures are more restricted than a full, ongoing partnership, the same basic laws apply.

Also worth noting about partnerships is that each partner can bind the partnership to legal contracts with third parties, either by having the express authority to do so, the implied authority to do so, or if the third party can reasonably have assumed that the partner had the *apparent* authority to do so. When partners engage in contracting agreements that go beyond their specified authority, it can get very sticky and sometimes lead to litigation. Once again, it's a strong argument for drafting a specific partnership agreement.

The third business form is a *corporation*. The formation of a corporation requires that formal articles of incorporation be filed with the state, that bylaws be adopted, and that the corporation hold organizational meetings in accordance with state laws. Depending on the state's law, a corporation can be formed by as few as one person. Ownership shares in a corporation are transferred through the buying and selling of stock, and termination occurs either through merger with another corporation or liquidation (selling off all assets, paying off creditors, and distributing the remainder to the stockholders). A corporation pays taxes on its income, and the stockholders also pay taxes on any dividends distributed from that income. The double taxation problem disappears if the corporation's directors designate it an *S Corporation*, in which case, for tax purposes, the income is passed directly through to the stockholders who claim it on their own personal returns.

From a legal standpoint, the key benefit of a corporation is that the corporate entity assumes the liability for any business debts. If, for example, Craig were to sue your corporation for breach of contract, should you lose the case, only the corporation would be liable and have to pay up. Craig would not be able to extract payment from your personal assets, such as your home or your personal bank accounts. This legal protection is the reason so many companies incorporate. However, be forewarned that, if a court determines that a corporation is merely a sham designed to hide assets from creditors, the court can do what's known as *piercing the corporate veil*, and, if it does that, creditors can go after an owner's personal assets as well as the corporate ones. For this reason, it's advisable that a corporation keep sufficient assets in its corporate accounts to cover its routine business debts.

Both partnerships and corporations have hybrid forms known as *limited partnerships, limited liability partnerships*, and *limited liability companies*.

The limited partnership—or LP, as it's abbreviated—is structured so that there is at least one *general partner* who controls the day-to-day operation and has personal liability for the partnership's debts; meanwhile, there are *limited partners* whose personal liability is limited to just that partner's financial investment in the LP. By contrast, a limited liability partnership—or LLP—has no general partner with personal liability, but, instead, each partner is personally responsible for his own acts or mistakes. In other words, if Craig successfully sues your partner for an illegality your partner personally committed on the job, your partner's personal assets might be at stake, but Craig might not be able to get at your personal assets.

The limited liability company—or LLC—is very popular nowadays in that it affords the limited liability protection of a corporation, can be formed by as few as one person, and allows for the pass-through taxation of a partnership. Like a corporation, an LLC must file formal documents with the state. Those include articles of organization and the adoption of an operating agreement that's similar to corporate bylaws. The LLC is terminated by unanimous agreement of its members or by the withdrawal or death of a member, and a member can only transfer his interest in the LLC with the unanimous consent of the other members.

Choosing a business form is an important decision, and it probably wouldn't hurt to consult legal and/or tax professionals about such things if you're not sure which is right for you.

So far, this discussion has focused on your art as a for-profit business. That's why each of the above discussions on form includes a comment about income taxes. But what if you're putting together an organization that's *not for profit*? Examples might be a literary society, a museum, or an orchestra. Each of these will likely involve some outlay of money, and perhaps some form of revenue in order to maintain itself. However, if revenue is generated for the purpose of covering operating expenses and not for the purpose of generating a profit for shareholders, then such an organization might qualify for tax-exempt status under the Internal Revenue Code § 501(c)(3).

First, let's understand what "nonprofit" means. It doesn't mean that everyone who works there has to do so for free. A nonprofit is entitled to pay staff and independent contractors for their work, as would any other business. However, the thing that separates a nonprofit from a for-profit business is that a nonprofit doesn't pay dividends to its owners. For example, if a theater company is a nonprofit, it can pay its artistic director a salary and benefits for the work that artistic director performs as an employee of the company, but it can't distribute profits to its board of directors as a for-profit would to its stockholders. (Do keep in mind that, just because that artistic director is working for a nonprofit, it doesn't mean the artistic director is exempt from paying income taxes on earnings. Anyone who earns money from labor performed for an employer—nonprofit or otherwise—is subject to paying taxes. It's only the nonprofit organization itself that can be exempted from that obligation.)

To qualify for tax-exempt status under Section 501(c)(3), the nonprofit must be a corporation, a trust, or an unincorporated association that is

> *organized and operated exclusively for religious, charitable, scientific, testing for public safety, literary, or educational purposes, or to foster national or international amateur sports competition (but only if no part of its activities involve the provision of athletic facilities or equipment), or for the prevention of cruelty to children or animals.*

For most arts related organizations, the tax-exempt purpose typically falls within the *literary* or *educational* categories, which can be relatively broad. (Just to provide a little context, the IRS website lists museums and symphony orchestras as examples of educational organizations.)

In addition to providing relief from the responsibility of paying income tax to the federal government, a 501(c)(3) designation might also help an organization attain exempt status from state taxes levied on income, sales, or property. But, remember, tax-exempt status is granted separately by the federal and state governments. Check your state laws to determine the procedures for getting state tax-exempt status.

Most organizations need to apply formally for tax-exempt status with the federal government by filing Form 1023 with the IRS. If the status is granted, there may also be some annual reporting requirements. For more information, the IRS provides a detailed and simple explanation in a document titled *Applying for 501(c)(3) Tax-Exempt Status*, available on its website at www.irs.gov.

What Can and Can't
the Artist Use?

Up till now we've been talking about what's yours—that is, the property that belongs to you, the artist. Our focus has been on what you possess and how you transact it in the business end of what you do. For the serious artist who aspires to be more than just a hobbyist, these are important things to know. It's important for anyone selling anything to know how his business works.

But now it's time to turn our attention to things that *aren't* yours—at least, not yours initially. I'm talking about the existing properties that an artist sometimes employs or incorporates into the creative process in order to give birth to a brand new work of art. The visual artist who makes a collage out of pieces of other people's photographs; the music artist who "samples" snippets of another musicians' riffs and edits them together into a new recording; the essayist who quotes passages from another writer's book; the painter who paints his own rendition of another painter's work; the producer who scores his film with another's musical compositions; the comic actor who parodies a television show through exaggerated mimicking of its characters and scenes—these are just a few examples of the many occasions when one artist appropriates the property of another.

You know from the number of lawsuits you hear about in the news—where someone's accusing someone else of misappropriating his intellectual property—that not everything in this world is fair game for the artist who wants to take a bit of this and borrow a bit of that to use as components of a new artistic creation. Sometimes these appropriations are legal. Sometimes they're not. Recognizing which among the intellectual property orchard are permissible pickings and which are forbidden fruit isn't always an easy task.

So let's try to take at least some of the mystery out of it by examining the laws that govern this.

Original Material and Factual Matter

The safest elements you can employ in the creation of art are those that are entirely original creations of yours. As we covered earlier, an artistic work doesn't necessarily have to be totally unique from every other pre-existing work to qualify for copyright protection. Even identical material can legally qualify so long as each work was the original brainchild of the artist and not just a copy of another work.

Suppose, for example, Angela is sitting on her front porch when, suddenly, out of the blue, a burst of inspiration comes over her, and she scribbles onto a paper napkin the following poem:

> *There once was a girl, name of Uma,*
> *Who boarded a train out of Yuma.*
> *She sampled the salsa,*
> *Then yelled clear to Tulsa,*
> *"Revenge is yours, O Montezuma!"*

Whether or not this verse is destined to become a classic, the fact that it sprang out of no place other than Angela's clever mind makes it a fully copyrightable piece of intellectual property that now belongs to her. Angela could publish it, set it to music, base a screenplay on it, or do anything else that copyright affords to the creator of an original work. If someone else were to acquire a copy of Angela's poem and try to publish it, set it to music, or whatever else, Angela would have grounds for a copyright infringement action against that copier. Her rights, as we know, take effect immediately as soon as the work is fixed in a tangible form of expression, and that fixation was accomplished when she scribbled the words onto a napkin. It matters not that Halsy may have composed something extremely similar, which she inked onto a tablecloth while sitting on her own front porch on the other side of the country. Nor would it matter if Halsy and Angela lived in the same part of the country or even in the same town—or, for that matter, even if they lived on the same block. It wouldn't matter even if they were inspired by watching the same train out of Yuma rumble past their homes. What's more, as was noted in an earlier chapter, when it comes to copyright, even if the two of them composed the exact same verse, right down to the spelling and punctuation, it still wouldn't change a thing. Angela's copyright claim isn't the least bit impacted by Halsy's own claim on the same compositional expression, and *vice versa*, so long as each of the two women came up with their creations independently, and neither copied the poem from the other.

Remember—copyright is the right to control how *copies* are made of your work; it's not the right to control other people's creative thought process. If an artist had to worry that the work he's creating might be too similar to one already created by someone else, and that the artist might then be sued over charges that he infringed a work he never even heard of, that could put a serious crimp in the willingness of artists to create new works. That, as we know, would be counter to the whole purpose of having copyright laws. Therefore, material that springs entirely from your own original thoughts is safe for you to use.

That doesn't mean you can simply claim ignorance of another person's work and walk away scot-fee from a copyright infringement rap where the infringement is fairly blatant. When dealing with longer, more substantial works, the odds of two people coming up with exactly the same expression are pretty slight. So courts are likely to take a long, hard look at two works that are almost identical. There are, of course, lots of occasions where people working completely independent of each other arrive at very similar ideas. Two people might, for example, come up with two very similar screenplays. (This isn't necessarily a farfetched hypothetical since it's been said in various circles that Hollywood basically makes the same six movies over and over. But we needn't dwell on that.) While basic plot points can never be copyrighted, the exact sequence of events and actuations can. Therefore, if one person claims another has copied substantial portions of and, therefore, infringed his screenplay, the court will look not at the basic plot—nor will it have to look for verbatim copying of exact language—but, instead, it will look at the specific scene-by-scene progression of the stories to determine similarities.

Not all similarities of plot will automatically be viewed as a copyright infringement. There's a doctrine known as *scenes a faire* that refers to those incidents, settings, or characters that are, for most practical matters, commonplace if not indispensible to a given topic. If you write a story about two people meeting and falling in love, you're not going to be able to copyright the plot development that they then get married. It's just too commonplace and obvious a development. *Scenes a faire* are not copyrightable because they're deemed to be elements that would naturally appear in similar works. However, if multiple particularities of one work are just too close to another's to be a mere coincidence, the courts could rule that it's copyright infringement. This is a "substantial similarity" standard employed and described by Judge Learned Hand of the U.S. Second Circuit Court of Appeals in the 1936 case, *Sheldon v. Metro-Goldwyn Pictures Corp.*, when he wrote, "it is enough that substantial parts were lifted." The same standard is also employed in cases involving infringement claims regarding other forms of media. For instance, where one artist's original visual creation has been copied by another visual artist so that the overall look of the copy resembles the work of the first artist, courts use an "ordinary observer test" or an "average lay observer test" to conclude if the general public would likely notice an infringing similarity.[14] In cases where a substantial similarity is detected, the conclusion that the second person copied from the first person is inferred, even if there's no eyewitness or direct evidence to prove the copying took place.

Music artist George Harrison got into trouble over just such an inference of unauthorized copying. It involved the ex-Beatle's composition of the song *My Sweet Lord*. As his many fans know, the recording of the song was a huge hit in the 1970s. The catchy melody might even be going through your head as you read this. And therein lies the pitfall into which Mr. Harrison stumbled. That catchy tune from *My Sweet Lord* also happened to be the melody of the song *He's So Fine*, which topped the charts in 1963 when the Chiffons released a recording of it. The result was *Bright Tunes Music Corp. v. Harrisongs Music*, the beginning of a twenty-year legal battle in which Mr. Harrison was accused of having plagiarized the earlier song. Having already had, by that time, a distinguished and profitable career as a composer, it would be hard to believe that Mr. Harrison felt the need to steal someone else's music. The court acknowledged that. However, the court also took into account that it was unlikely Mr. Harrison had never before heard the recording of *He's So Fine* while it was getting wide distribution and play

---

14   Some courts use the "ordinary observer test" and some use the "average lay observer test" when handling copyright infringement claims regarding visual arts. Basically, the "ordinary observer test" focuses on the differences between the two works and whether an ordinary observer would detect those differences or overlook them. If an ordinary observer would detect the differences, then a substantial similarity is not proved. By contrast, the "average lay observer test" proves substantial similarity when an average lay observer would recognize the elements that were appropriated by one from the other. From a practical standpoint, the "ordinary observer test" is more favorable for the defendant being accused of misappropriation, and the "average lay observer test" is more favorable for the plaintiff alleging that his work has been infringed.

during the days when it was a hit song, and Mr. Harrison admitted as much. So, although no one supposes that he had deliberately attempted to commit copyright infringement, the court inferred that Mr. Harrison must have inadvertently plagiarized the earlier song whose melody resided somewhere in his subconscious memory. In winning their case, the plaintiffs didn't need to prove Mr. Harrison deliberately attempted to infringe their intellectual property. They needed only to show a substantial similarity between the two songs, and that the defendant had access to the earlier work.

The moral of the story is don't count on pleading ignorance to get you off the hook if what you've created isn't really your own creation but just a slightly modified version of someone else's. The courts won't necessarily take your word for it that you didn't copy the protected elements of another's work.

Elements that are always fair game for the artist to raid legally are raw facts and data. No one can copyright a fact. Even if you're the first person to discover a fact, you still can't lay a copyright claim to it. The fact that Pluto was downgraded in 2006 from a planet in our solar system is not something the first author to write about it can copyright and prevent all other writers from repeating. To do so would be to render all but the very first author's book on the subject factually inaccurate. Obviously, that can't be allowed to happen, as it would be a disservice to society as a whole.

Compilations of facts might be copyrightable. The way in which the data is culled, organized, and presented could be copyright-protected as an original work. However, the facts within those compilations are free for anyone to use. An example of this would be the listings in a telephone directory. The listings are a mere mechanical compilation of names, addresses, and phone numbers, and the alphabetizing of the names is hardly an original thought. If anything, an alphabetical listing is purely inevitable in such directories. Therefore, the data found in a standard telephone directory is not copyrightable. However, if someone were to select listings based on a particular set of criteria and present them in an atypical arrangement (perhaps featuring only businesses owned by a particular group of people or featuring certain categories of business services not ordinarily found in a standard directory), that might be sufficiently original to acquire copyright protection.

The same would apply to statistics. A baseball player's batting average, for instance, can't be copyrighted. It's a fact that anyone with the ability to do simple arithmetic could calculate. Therefore, the manufacturer of a set of baseball cards might be able to copyright the design and presentation of the statistics on the card, but not the statistics themselves.

History is a prime example of factual matter that cannot be copyrighted. If you write a screenplay about George Washington and his famous crossing of the Delaware River, that's a historical happening, not a concoction of your own imagination. As such, you can't copyright the storyline so far as it's a dramatization of what actually took place. You could copyright the wording you use to tell the story. That's a particular expression that is copyrightable. However, beyond that, history is up for grabs by anyone who wants to make use of it.

But, you ask, what about those who use history as a mere springboard to stories that contain elements that aren't confirmed in the history books as absolute facts and might, in short, be a mixture of fact and fancy? What if, for example, that Washington-crossing-the-Delaware screenplay contains a scene in which the writer suggests that it wasn't General Washington who planned the battle at Trenton, but, rather, it was the regiment's cook? I suppose such a happening could have been possible, but there's no certifiable evidence of this that I'm aware of. So, if the screenwriter puts this into the script, is it a copyrightable element that no one else can copy?

This raises an interesting point. Does history need to be *provable* to make it freely usable without the user fearing he'll be accused of infringing the copyright of a pre-existing work referencing the same alleged bit of possible history?

To help answer this, I'll cite a couple of cases that dealt with this very issue. The first is *Hoehling v. Universal City Studios*. The case involved two retellings of the story of the fateful last voyage of the dirigible *Hindenburg*. The dirigible, as we all know, burst into flames without warning or apparent reason while it was docking in Lakehurst, New Jersey, in 1937. Since then, there has been much speculation about what actually happened to the *Hindenburg*. Years after the accident, A.A. Hoehling wrote a book based on his own research of the tragedy, and in his book he theorized that one of the *Hindenburg's* crew members was responsible for the deliberate sabotage of the dirigible. Keep in mind that Mr. Hoehling's conclusions were his *theory* based on the evidence he collected, not irrefutable facts.

About a decade after Mr. Hoehling's book came out, another author, Michael MacDonald Mooney, published a book on the *Hindenburg* disaster.

This second book, described as a bit more literary than historical, once again suggested that the same crew member was responsible for sabotaging the craft. Mr. Mooney admitted to using Mr. Hoehling's book as a reference material. When Mr. Mooney's book was adapted into a screenplay and the production company announced plans to release the film, Mr. Hoehling sued, alleging that the latter works amounted to copyright infringement because they misappropriated key plot points from his earlier book. The Second Circuit Court of Appeals disagreed with Mr. Hoehling. In its ruling, the court said, "To avoid a chilling effect on authors who contemplate tackling an historical issue or event, broad latitude must be granted to subsequent authors who make use of historical subject matter, including theories or plots." The theory that was at the core of the works about the *Hindenburg* was one that was based entirely on the interpretation of historical facts. Anyone is free to interpret such facts and draw conclusions. Therefore, the interpretations and conclusions can't be copyrighted, regardless of who is first to draw those conclusions.

The second case, *Nash v. CBS*, involved a story about the infamous gangster, John Dillinger. Jay Robert Nash wrote a book in which he concluded from his research that Dillinger wasn't gunned down in front of a Chicago movie theater in 1934 but, rather, survived and was living on the west coast as late as 1979. When CBS later broadcast an episode of its program *Simon and Simon* that featured a story about Dillinger having avoided being gunned down in 1934 and living on the west coast, Mr. Nash sued. Again the studio admitted to having appropriated material from the author's book, and again the court (this time the Seventh Circuit Court of Appeals) ruled against the author. The rationale was that Mr. Nash hadn't portrayed his book as fiction. If it had been fiction, the elements of it would be original products of his own imagination and copyrightable. Instead, he portrayed it as a theory based on factual evidence. Although the theory might be wrong, it also might be right, and, if it's correct, then it's history. As the court noted, "the first person to conclude that Dillinger survived does not get dibs on history."

Now perhaps you're thinking this sounds like a bum deal for the original authors. They did all the work of sifting through the evidence, hypothesizing possibilities, and drawing conclusions. The Johnny-Come-Lately people got a free ride on all that initial labor. Hardly seems fair, does it? However, I remind you that copyright doesn't reward labor; it rewards originality.

Public Domain Property

Nothing lasts forever, and that includes copyright. Lengthy though the current laws make its duration, eventually the copyright on anything will expire, and the work will fall into the *public domain*. That's a domain in which, like the caution from the famous Victor Herbert/Glenn MacDonough song about Toyland, "once you pass its borders, you can never return again." Once a work passes into the public domain, its copyright disappears permanently and it's free for anyone to use.[15] That is, you can take public domain material and republish it, repurpose it, or change it into a derivative work—all without having to ask anyone's permission. You don't have to pay anyone or ask for a license to produce *Hamlet*. The play is hundreds of years old, and any protections it might have had—if, indeed, there ever were any—are long since gone. You also don't need to ask any descendents of Thomas Nast if it's okay for you to draw a copy of his iconic Santa Claus cartoons that were published in 19th century newspapers. Mr. Nast is long dead and so are any copyrights that he might have held on his work. You could get into a world of trouble if you draw your own copy and then try to pass it off as an authentic work of the original artist (that's forgery, my friends), but you won't be violating copyright law if you simply create your own rendition closely resembling it. What's more, if you want to make a recording of yourself singing the aforementioned *Toyland*, it's a song that's now free for the taking, having passed the borders into the public domain some time ago. (That doesn't necessarily mean that other recordings of *Toyland* are in the public domain. Chances are they're not. It only means that the song itself—the musical notation and lyrics as published by its authors in 1903—is now public domain material. This is an important distinction and one that shouldn't be overlooked.)

As we noted earlier, United States copyright laws have changed over the years, and the duration of copyright has been extended, from the original fourteen years with a renewal of another fourteen, to the current term of the

---

15   There is a sort of exception to the rule, but it doesn't apply to works created in the United States. If a work was once considered to be public domain material in America only because it didn't comply with the formalities of U.S. law, or the nation of origin of that work didn't have a copyright agreement with this country, the Uruguay Round Agreements Act restored the protections observed for those works here as of 1996. But part of that agreement was that works were only eligible for copyright restoration if they had a current copyright in effect in their nation of origin. Congress officially made the terms of the agreement part of the American copyright laws as 17 U.S.C. § 104A.

life of the creator plus an additional seventy years (or a total of ninety-five to 120 years for works made for hire or anonymous/pseudonymous works). Because different laws applied at different times, there isn't one clear, simple rule that dictates when a work falls into the public domain. But, because this is important, let's try to make some sense out of it. Take a deep breath and try to stay with me...

We'll start with the easy ones—the moldy oldies.

When it comes to public domain property, the magic year is 1922. Anything that was published in the year 1922 or earlier is past the point of copyright protection, and it's in the public domain, free for you to do with what you will. Knock yourself out.

Beginning with January 1, 1923, things start to get a little more complicated.

The first thing you have to remember is that, prior to 1978, American copyright law was governed by the Copyright Act of 1909. That act measured the duration of copyright not by the author's life but by the work's publication date, or its date of registration if registered with the Copyright Office in unpublished form. The 1909 Act defined "date of publication" with the following language:

> *the earliest date when copies of the first authorized edition were*
> *placed on sale, sold, or publicly distributed by the proprietor of*
> *the copyright or under his authority.*

It doesn't matter whether the work was sold for a profit or just given away for free so long as copies were made available to at least some portion of the general public. There were also some cases that defined the public display of some works, such as paintings or sculptures, as a form of publication under the copyright statute. Therefore, to determine the effective copyright duration of a work created between 1923 and 1977, you need to know if and when it was published or, in the alternative, when it was registered with the Copyright Office.

The second thing to keep in mind about the old law is that the duration of a copyright lasted twenty-eight years from the date it was secured, with the option for a renewal of another twenty-eight years. Under that law, the copyright holder needed to apply for the renewal before the first term expired. If the renewal application wasn't filed, the copyright expired after the first term. A lot of works entered the public domain early as a result of neglect or indifference regarding the filing for renewal.

The third thing to note is that placing a notice of copyright on the work wasn't optional under the 1909 law. The notice had to be there or else copyright protections could be forfeited. There was a provision in the law that forgave an innocent mistake that inadvertently omitted the copyright notice, thus making the status of such works even more difficult to nail down. In essence, though, this is yet another thing that needs to be researched and taken into account when determining whether a work published before 1978 is in the public domain.

When the current law came into effect, works existing under the old law that had already had their copyrights renewed (and were then in their second term) had that second term expanded from twenty-eight to sixty-seven years, thereby making their full duration of copyright protection a total of ninety-five years.

For works that were still in their first copyright term when the new law took effect, the second term was also extended to sixty-seven years, for a total protection of ninety-five years. However, those works that were copyrighted between January 1, 1950, and December 31, 1963, were required to have a renewal application on file to qualify for the extension. Whereas, works copyrighted between January 1, 1964, and December 31, 1977, were not required to have filed a renewal. The renewal on the latter group vested automatically after the end of the twenty-eighth year of their first term.

Are your eyes glazing over yet? There's more.

If a work was in existence but hadn't been published or copyrighted by January 1, 1978, it was automatically given full protection under the current copyright law—that is, life plus seventy years, or the 95/120-year duration, whichever was appropriate. The law specified that, in no case would the copyright on such works expire before December 31, 2002, and, if those works were published before that date, the copyright protection would be extended another forty-five years, running through the end of 2047.

Okay, have you had enough of the statutory rigmarole? Let's just recap with only the most basic rules of thumb regarding when a work's in the public domain:

- Published *before* 1923, it's in the public domain.
- Published with proper notice *between* 1964 and 1977, the copyright protection's automatic. It's *not* in the public domain.
- Created *after* 1977, the copyright protection's automatic. It's *not* in the public domain (even if it was never published).

- Published with proper notice *between* the years 1923 through 1963—this is the "iffy" zone. Whether a work published during this period is still copyright protected or has fallen into the public domain depends on whether the copyright owner renewed the initial copyright before it expired.

To check on whether a work's copyright under the old laws was renewed, you need to search the records of the Copyright Office. You can do it online for some copyright records—the ones that were registered or renewed since January 1, 1978. The Copyright Office has those records in an online database, available at www.copyright.gov/records. Among its entries, it includes all the renewals of works published between 1950 and 1963. The database doesn't include works that were published between 1923 and 1949, and the search for those must be done elsewhere. The Copyright Office provides a *Catalogue of Copyright Entries* that allows for manual perusal of all registrations from 1891 through 1978. That catalogue is available at the Copyright Office in Washington, D.C., and it's also often available at major libraries around the United States. If you're unable to get to Washington, and your local library doesn't have a copy of the *Catalogue of Copyright Entries*, you can always hire someone else to do the search for you. Additionally, you can pay the Copyright Office to do the search.[16]

Here it's important to throw in a special caution. Just because one part of a work is in the public domain doesn't necessarily mean that all parts of it are. Sometimes there's a hidden copyright protection lurking beneath the surface of a public domain work. Let's look at an example.

In *Russell v. Price*, the United States Court of Appeals for the Ninth Circuit was presented with a case that involved a 1938 movie adaptation of George Bernard Shaw's play, *Pygmalion*. The film's copyright was allowed to expire in 1966. However, Mr. Shaw had registered the copyright for his play in 1913 and renewed it in 1944. Under the term extension then allowed, the copyright on the play wasn't scheduled to expire until 1988. In the 1970s, someone acquired and attempted to distribute the film that had fallen into the public domain. The people who then owned the copyright on the play filed a lawsuit to stop the unlicensed distribution of the movie. The court ruled that, although the film itself was a public domain property, the underlying

---

16 As of this writing, the Copyright Office was charging $165.00 per hour to conduct a search of registration records.

play was not. The film was a derivative of the original play, and a derivative's own copyright extends only to new material contained exclusively in the derivative, not to the matter contained in the underlying work. Because exhibiting the film would necessitate exhibiting parts of Mr. Shaw's play—a play that was still protected by copyright—an unauthorized exhibition of the film would be tantamount to an unauthorized exhibition of the play. The latter was not permissible under copyright law. As such, the court ruled that the plaintiffs could stop the defendants from distributing the film without their permission.

One last thing while we're on the subject...by law, the United States government cannot claim a copyright on anything it creates.[17] A pamphlet produced by a federal agency or photographs taken by a federal employee within the scope of his employment—just to give a couple of examples— are works that immediately fall into the public domain, and anyone can use them. However—you just knew there was gonna be a "however," didn't you?—the U.S. government is not precluded from receiving and holding a copyright that has been transferred to it. For example, if that photographer were an independent contractor rather than a federal employee, and the photos weren't a work made for hire but, rather, were simply part of the photographer's stock, then the photographer would own the copyright on them. If the photographer later sells those photos to the federal government, and he also sells with the photos all of their intellectual property rights, the government will have purchased the copyright on the images as well as the images, themselves. In this case, the federal government would own the copyrights, and the photos would not be part of the public domain.

Okay, so copyright law isn't as simple as you might have wished for. But, if you wanted an easy profession, you wouldn't have become an artist. Right?

Fair Use

Perhaps, by now, you're thinking to yourself that there's just no way you'll ever try to incorporate into your art anything that anyone else ever created, because traipsing about the copyright minefield is just too dangerous. And the last thing you need is to step into a legal sinkhole that could leave

---

17   This is mandated by 17 U.S.C. § 105.

you on the defending end of an infringement suit. For that matter, you might be wondering how anybody ever dares risk it at all. You know you've seen such things out there—one artist appropriating portions of what appears to be the intellectual property of another—and you know that at least some of that appropriated material must be under the protection of the All-Powerful Copyright. So how do they do it?

Well, my friends, despite its mighty and far-reaching powers, there's one chink in the copyright armor. It's called the *fair use doctrine*. Even if a work is fully protected by copyright, and even if the person who holds that copyright is disinclined to give permission for anyone else to use parts of the work, under the fair use doctrine there are occasions when portions of a copyrighted work can be legally appropriated by someone else. Section 107 of the Copyright Act defines the limitations on a copyright holder's exclusive rights with the following language:

> *the fair use of a copyrighted work, including such use by repro-duction in copies or phonorecords or by any other means speci-fied by [the sections of the Act defining the exclusive rights in copyrighted works], for purposes such as criticism, comment, news reporting, teaching (including multiple copies for class-room use), scholarship, or research, is not an infringement of copyright.*

In other words, when done correctly and for the proper purposes, the appro-priation of someone else's intellectual property is considered a fair use exception to copyright—in essence, a safe harbor from copyright infringe-ment claims. The key to docking in that harbor is understanding what con-stitutes a legally proper use of someone else's work.

You'll note that educational and research purposes are among the occa-sions listed in the statute. For instance, a teacher making photocopies of a magazine article to hand out to all the students in class as part of the day's lesson would be a fair use. Obviously, there's a benefit to society as a whole when formal education is allowed to proceed without certain intellectual roadblocks. There's also a special provision in the Copyright Act (Section 108) that allows a fair use exception for libraries and archives to make repro-ductions of the works in their collections.

Also in the statute's list is *news reporting*. The nation's long-stand-ing tradition of a free press requires that the news media be able to excerpt things about which they're referencing. If, for example, a television news program is reporting on the anniversary of Martin Luther King Jr.'s "I Have a Dream" speech, it serves everyone's interest if the program can play a portion of the filmed speech as part of the news coverage. For this purpose, the station's broadcasting of an excerpt of that copyright protected speech is a fair use. However, the same TV station could probably not claim a fair use exception if it broadcast the exact same excerpt as part of a drama. A drama is not the same as *bona fide news reporting*. In this case, excerpting the speech is just appropriating copyrighted material for whatever entertainment value the producers of the drama feel it will add. Entertainment alone is not one of the purposes enumerated in the fair use statute. Additionally, a documentary about Dr. King is unlikely to be viewed as news reporting, either. Informative though they often are, documentaries are not the coverage of current events and issues of concern that constitute what are typically viewed as the day's *news*.

Another big part of the fair use doctrine is what's referred to as *fair comment and criticism*. Imagine a movie review where the critic can't tell us anything specific about the plot of the film or show us a clip. Or imagine a book review where the reviewer can't quote a passage from the book. Such limitations would greatly diminish the value of the reviews and would seriously infringe on the reviewers' freedom of speech. A person commenting on or criticizing a work often needs to be able to excerpt a sufficient amount of the work in order to give the critique the necessary context. Hence, comment and criticism are purposes for which a fair use exception to copyright is allowed.

But what about this case? Let's say Chris writes for a magazine, and he somehow gets hold of an advance copy of Julieta's tell-all book about her life as a famous stunt pilot. Although the book's not due to be released to the public for another month, the magazine publishes Chris's article about the book, giving away the major moments in the book's storyline and excerpting various passages of the text as direct quotations. Julieta and her publisher are peeved to see this premature disclosure of what they had hoped would be a best-seller. Now the key selling points of the book are already revealed, and the book doesn't even hit the shelves for another month. Is Chris's article a fair use?

To make these kinds of calls, Section 107 of the Copyright Act provides the following factors to be considered:

- What is the purpose and character of the work appropriating the copyrighted material, and is that appropriation for commercial or for nonprofit educational purposes?
- What is the nature of the copyrighted material being appropriated?
- What is the amount and substantiality of the portion of the appropriated material in relation to the copyrighted work as a whole?
- What effect will the work appropriating the copyrighted material have on the potential market for or value of the work from which the material was taken?

Let's go through these factors in regard to our hypothetical situation and see how they might apply.

First, when analyzing the magazine's purpose and character, Chris might claim that what he wrote was a form of news reporting, which is one of the purposes for which fair use exceptions are allowed. However, the purposes referenced in the statute aren't carte blanche to appropriate as much as one wants and do whatever one wants with it. Within that framework of fair use opportunities, the above four factors must still be assessed and weighed to determine whether the use was fair. If a court were deliberating this case, it would take into account that the article's content might be considered news and then move on to weigh the criterion regarding whether that news coverage was of a commercial or noncommercial nature. There's probably little doubt that the magazine publishing Chris's article is a publication of a commercial nature, and a commercial exploitation of another's property tends to weigh against a finding of fair use. Allowing someone to profit from another's work without paying the customary price is not the motive behind the fair use doctrine.

Second, we look at the nature of the work from which the copyrighted material was appropriated. Julieta's book is a nonfiction telling of her life story, and, as we know, historical facts aren't copyrightable. Those passages that Chris lifted, which relate only to *facts* about things that actually happened, will weigh in favor of a fair use ruling. However, if Chris's article also took subjective material from the book—things that aren't simply history—that could weigh against fair use. Another "nature of the work" factor in Julieta's favor is that the book is, as yet, unpublished, and the author's right to control the first public distribution of her creative expression weighs against others being able to use it before its official release.

Third, the amount and the substantiality of the appropriated material is a factor of significance to be deliberated. Did Chris copy a significant amount of Julieta's book; or, in the alternative, was the substance of the copied portions of such significance that they constituted the very heart of the book? If either of these things is true, it would weigh in favor of Julieta's infringement claim. If neither could be said of Chris's article, it would weigh in Chris's favor.

Fourth, and perhaps most significantly, one has to examine what impact the premature publication of the appropriated material will have on the value and marketability of the copyrighted work. What effect will Chris's article have on Julieta's ability to sell her book? Will the market for such a book dwindle after the key passages within it have already been revealed to the magazine's readership? If the answer to this is yes, then it will weigh heavily in favor of Julieta's side and against Chris's claim of fair use.

As stated above, the amount, and sometimes the proportional amount, of material appropriated from a copyrighted work is one of the considerations that must be taken into account in cases debating whether someone's use of copyrighted material is a fair use or an infringement. Because it's a quantifiable test with measurable amounts, it might be looked upon as one of the easier fair use tests. However, it's not nearly as clear-cut as a lot of people seem to imagine. I can't tell you how many times I've heard someone state their earnest belief that there's some magic percentage of a work that you're allowed to use without fear of committing copyright infringement. Oh!—what a simple world it would be if only there were such a bright-line standard by which to make the judgment calls. But I assure you there is *no such thing as a fair use maximum word count or percentage.*

There is a fair use doctrine that's known as *de minimis.* It applies to the appropriation of such a small portion of a copyrighted work as to be an immaterial usage that doesn't constitute infringement. However, the *de minimis* standard is a moving target. It does not dictate an exact percentage of the work, or an exact number of words, or an exact number of musical notes that are fair game for others to take. And, if someone tries to tell you otherwise, I dispute that notion with what I'll call *Exhibit A*: the case of *Elsmere Music v. National Broadcasting Company.*

The *Elsmere Music* case involved the appropriation of a portion of the song *I Love New York*, made famous by the State of New York's tourism ad campaign of the 1970s. If you're old enough to remember it, you

probably remember it as the lyric phrase "I----------- love New Yo--------
----rk" repeated again and again to a four-note sequence that was part of a
larger, more complete song. NBC's popular *Saturday Night Live* program
appropriated that four-note melody and fashioned it into "I love Sodom" as
part of a comedic sketch about an ad campaign to improve the image of the
biblical city of Sodom. Elsmere Music, which owned the copyright on *I Love
New York*, took exception and filed suit against NBC for copyright infringement. Now keep in mind that *Saturday Night Live* appropriated only four
notes out of the full song's 100 measures and copied only two words from
its forty-five-word lyrics. (And the words, "I love," could hardly be called
a truly original lyrical combination.) Yet, despite that rather paltry taking,
a federal court in New York did *not* see this as a *de minimis* appropriation,
because, as the court put it, "the musical phrase that the lyrics 'I Love New
York' accompany, is the heart of the composition." The court added, "Use
of such a significant (albeit less than extensive) portion of the composition is
far more than merely a *De minimis* taking."

Now, if the appropriation of a mere four notes and two extremely common words doesn't automatically constitute *de minimis* under the fair use
doctrine, then I'm not inclined to recommend to anyone that they take anything for granted when it comes to the *de minimis* standard. As a lawyer
writing a general purpose guide such as this book, I can't advise you in this
text as to your particular situation should a question arise about the amount
you're able to appropriate from someone else's copyright-protected work.
But I encourage you to heed the lesson of the *Elsmere Music* case and understand that a *de minimis* defense to a copyright infringement charge will be
subject to a very fact-specific ruling should it go to court. And, remember,
it's not what *you* think is *de minimis*—it's what the *judge* thinks that counts.

Okay, so now that we know that NBC's *de minimis* defense didn't work,
who can tell me why NBC won the case?

Huh? *Won* the case? But wasn't their defense blown out of the water?

True, the *de minimis* claim didn't carry the day for NBC in the *Elsmere
Music* case, but another defense did—*parody*.

From a legal standpoint, parody falls under the *fair comment and criticism* prong of the fair use doctrine. One method of commenting on and
criticizing something is to parody it with humorous exaggeration or the like.
Poking fun at a political figure by mimicking that figure's way of talking or
behaving can have the effect of indirectly letting the world know what you

think of that politician. In the case of *Saturday Night Live's* parody of the *I Love New York* song, it was a tongue-in-cheek attempt to comment on the slick ad campaign the state was running and which featured the song as its anthem. Therefore, the song parody was a fair use.

Be forewarned that parody has its limits. A parody may appropriate only so much of the source material as is necessary to conjure to the minds of its audience that which is being parodied. You can't simply make wholesale, substantial appropriation of a copyrighted work in order to take a few humorous jabs at it. I realize that this isn't the most precise definition you could have hoped for in helping you to determine what's an acceptable appropriation for parody and what's too much. But, as I've said, rulings of this kind typically depend on a fact specific analysis. One court found *Your Show of Shows'* parody of the film *From Here to Eternity* to be a fair use[18], while another court found Jack Benny's parody of the film *Gaslight* to be copyright infringement based on the quantity of material it had appropriated[19].

While we're here, it's important for us to take a few moments to distinguish the difference between parody and satire. Most of us use the terms parody and satire as interchangeable synonyms. However, the law makes a major distinction between them. A *parody* pokes fun at the source material of what's being appropriated. In other words, if you're attempting to comment amusingly on the musical *Hello, Dolly!*, and you sing the title song with altered lyrics to lampoon the musical's big number, that's a parody. But if instead you're attempting to make an amusing critique of a famous corporation, and you set comical lyrics to that same *Hello, Dolly!* melody, that might not be parody under the legal definition. It's *satire*, which the law defines as a lampooning not of the source material being appropriated but, rather, of something other than the source material. Because satire doesn't comment on the material it's appropriating, satire doesn't count as a fair use of that material, and, without permission to use the source material, the satirist could be found guilty of copyright infringement.

Under any form of fair use, the appropriating party needs to undertake some sort of *transformative* use of the source material. That is, the new

---

18   *Columbia Pictures Corp. v. National Broadcasting Co.* (U.S. District Court, Southern District of California, 1955).

19   *Benny v. Loew's Inc.,* (9th Circuit Court of Appeals, 1956).

work must add something new and have a purpose that differs and doesn't just attempt to supersede the purpose of the original work. Simple duplication for the same purpose is just copyright infringement, whereas, if what's copied alters the original with new meaning, message, or expression, that's a transformative purpose of the work. A transformative purpose isn't a guarantee that a work will be declared a fair use. However, as the U.S. Supreme Court has ruled, the more transformative a new work is of its source material, the less other fair use factors will weigh against it.[20]

An illustrative case, *Blanch v. Koons*, came before the United States Court of Appeals for the Second Circuit in 2006. Visual artist Jeff Koons was commissioned to create a large-scale painting for exhibition in a German art gallery. Mr. Koons, whose work is sometimes referred to as "appropriation art," incorporated into his collage image a photo of a woman's legs that he electronically scanned from the pages of a magazine. Photographer Andrea Blanch recognized the legs in Mr. Koons' work as being part of a photo she had taken, and she sued for copyright infringement. On at least three prior occasions, Mr. Koons lost when he was taken to court over similar misappropriation charges. However, on this occasion, the court ruled in his favor. The court stated that, while it had previously "declined to find a transformative use when the defendant has done no more than find a new way to exploit the creative virtues of the original work," it determined that Mr. Koons' use of Ms. Blanch's photo went well beyond simply plopping a copyright protected image into his own art. The key elements that persuaded the court were that Mr. Koons (1) changed the colors of the image, (2) changed the background, (3) utilized a different medium (painting as opposed to photography), (4) dramatically changed the size, (5) altered the details of the objects in the image (including repositioning the orientation of the woman's legs and adding a heel to one of the feet), and (6) had an "entirely different purpose and meaning" for his work (a "commentary on the social and aesthetic consequences of mass media"). While Ms. Blanch could still recognize her own work in the new piece, in the court's eyes that work had been sufficiently transformed into something different—something that was a fair use.

---

20 If you're curious as to in which case the Supreme Court made this ruling, it was *Campbell v. Acuff-Rose Music*, in which the group 2 Live Crew was sued over its parody of Roy Orbison's signature song, *Oh, Pretty Woman*. 2 Live Crew proved its parody was a transformative use and won the case.

Real People

Have you ever come across someone whose life story was so interesting that you said to yourself, "That'd make a great book (or movie, or play, or ballad song, or whatever)"? Or maybe you encountered a news story about someone who did something fascinating, and that got your creative juices flowing, and you thought you might turn that person's personal history into an artistic expression of your own devising. Hey, you're an artist—and art imitates life, right? And reality is quite often the inspiration for artistic works, isn't it? Of course. Happens all the time. Sometimes art depicts people or events as they actually were, and sometimes it fictionalizes them. *Inherit the Wind* is a drama based on a fictionalized retelling of the famous Scopes "Monkey Trial" of 1925. The lawyer characters in the play are named Matthew Harrison Brady and Henry Drummond, but we all know they're representative of the real life adversaries in the Scopes case, William Jennings Bryan and Clarence Darrow.

You've probably seen those TV shows that feature a disclaimer that you just know some lawyer wrote and that states something along the lines of:

> *The following program is fictional. The characters in it do not represent any real people, living or dead, and the events depicted are in no way connected with or meant to imply any real happening you might have read about in the New York Times on April 17th, page 5, column 3, about half way down, right above the fold. We never saw or heard of that article. For that matter, we never even heard of the New York Times.*

The producers don't throw in that disclaimer because they're afraid of being sued by the *New York Times* for stealing the facts of a news article as the idea for a TV show. Facts aren't copyrightable, remember? Rather, what they're trying to head off is possible litigation by a real person who believes, rightly or wrongly, that the show's depiction of him gives him grounds for legal action against the producers. Even though historical happenings and facts are not copyrightable and, as such, are fair game for an artist to incorporate into his art, copyright isn't the only law on the books. What's more, it's certainly not the only law that matters when you're dealing with publicizing the facts of other people's lives. There are some legal restrictions that apply when the subject matter you're using involves real people. Those restrictions come from two key rights that everyone possesses: the *right of privacy* and the *right of publicity.*

The right of privacy is every individual's privilege to keep certain aspects of his personal life out of the public eye. While your brother might not mind your writing a book about his adventure climbing to the peak of Mount Kilimanjaro (about which he has told everyone, shown countless photos, and alerted the news media), he might not be so keen on your writing a book about the nervous breakdown he suffered when he learned that his wife was having an affair with her secretary (a topic about which he has told no one outside the immediate family). It may be true that the latter scenario is simply an accurate statement of facts from an actual happening—something that can't be protected by copyright law. However, apart from copyright, the disclosure of private facts about a person could be subject to restriction if that disclosure could be deemed to be highly offensive to a person of reasonable sensibilities. That is, if what's being disclosed is of such a shocking nature that it causes humiliation and emotional injury to the subject of the disclosed material, courts will weigh that in determining whether the disclosure has stepped over the bounds of what's legally acceptable.

The counterweight against which the "highly offensive" standard is measured is one known as *legitimate public concern.* The question that must be asked is whether the factual material is sufficiently related to a topic on which there's a legitimate public concern and whether that concern outweighs any emotional distress the disclosure of those facts might cause. In the case of your brother, do we really have a genuine public concern regarding your brother's situation? Or is it just an unnecessary, sensationalistic, morbid, and hurtful curiosity that leads us to read about his personal misfortune? Sometimes courts talk about a legitimate public *interest* rather than *concern.* To me, semantically, this seems like a lower hurdle to clear. I might have an interest in something without it necessarily being a major concern in my life. Yet the essence of it remains basically the same—the revelation of someone else's embarrassing life history, which has no connection to a public interest, is potentially legally dangerous.

In this age of blogging, Twittering, Facebooking, YouTubing, sexting, and send-us-your-amateur-pornography websites, you might wonder if privacy has become an irrelevancy and if there's anything really private left in this world that a person of reasonable sensibilities would consider to be a "highly offensive" revelation. But undoubtedly there are some intimate details that people would rather not make public knowledge. A person's sexual practices, for example, might be just such an intimate detail, as might also be a long-past indiscretion or criminal behavior. Or what about a private individual's failure of a drug test? There might be a reasonable explanation for that failure—perhaps prescription medicine caused a false positive result in the testing—but does that person want to have to explain that to everyone he knows if the test failure is disclosed to the public? "Even people who have nothing rationally to be ashamed of can be mortified by the publication of intimate details of their life," wrote Chief Judge Richard Posner of the Seventh Circuit Court of Appeals. "Most people in no way deformed or disfigured would nevertheless be deeply upset if nude photographs of themselves were published in a newspaper or a book."[21] In the absence of that legitimate public concern or interest we've been talking about, disclosing such things about another person, who's not okay with their disclosure, could land you in court for invasion of privacy.

The arena might be a bit different for public figures—people who have thrust themselves into the public eye and, as such, become people whose lives and habits are of concern or interest to the general public. Hilary Clinton, for example, might not enjoy the privilege of keeping the details of her life as private as, say, your brother can. (Unless, of course, your brother is Bill Clinton.) In the case of public figures, their own celebrity often makes newsworthy to a mass audience things that the rest of us do without arousing the slightest interest in even our nearest neighbors. But that doesn't mean that it's open season on every minute, personal detail about a public figure. Publishing Ms. Clinton's Social Security number, just to throw out an example, might be over the line and into the realm of disclosing private information for which there's no compelling concern for the public at large.

"Ah, but what if I *fictionalize* the person I'm modeling my character on?" you ask. "Surely, if I change the name to 'Melanie Blinton,' then no one can accuse me of infringing anyone's right to privacy."

Well, not necessarily. While fictionalizing a real person helps, it's not an absolute guarantee that you'll avoid a lawsuit. Even in a work of fiction, if people who know the real person on whom your character is based would be able to recognize that person in your character, then you haven't truly disguised the real person enough to avoid legal troubles should that real person take umbrage at the way you've portrayed him. Also, keep in mind that the

---

21   Chief Judge Posner wrote that in the 1993 published opinion of *Haynes v. Alfred A. Knopf.*

whole world doesn't necessarily have to be able to identify the real person you've modeled your character on. It's enough if the people who know that person would be able to recognize his persona in the character you've created. If Ms. Clinton and her friends take one look at what you've created and say, *"Melanie Blinton, my foot! That's Hilary!"*—then you might want to start working on a darn good explanation for why you felt the public desperately needed to know her Social Security number.

As I said, Ms. Clinton's right of privacy is somewhat curtailed by her public figure status. Not so with regard to her *right of publicity*. In fact, as a public figure, she arguably has an even greater stake in guarding her right of publicity than do most people who aren't household names. The right of publicity, you see, is every person's right to control how his own name or likeness is used for commercial exploitation. This particular right tends to strike almost everyone as a perfectly reasonable doctrine—at least, when it's your own name or likeness that's being exploited. If someone's using your image to help market something, doesn't it stand to reason that you ought to get some form of compensation for helping sell it? In addition, shouldn't you be able to put a stop to it if someone's using your image without your permission to sell something you either don't make any money on or that you're not all that thrilled to be associated with? (How many men would willingly appear in those ads for erectile dysfunction treatment pills if they weren't getting paid for it?)

More often than not, the people who are pitching products or services are professional actors or models who've negotiated a deal for the commercial utilization of their images or voices. But sometimes someone tries to capitalize on the celebrity of a public figure by incorporating unauthorized images or recordings of the celebrity into a commercial exploitation; and here is where the public figures have a strong case to make against those who appropriate their marketable likenesses for exploitations to which the celebrity didn't consent. There have been a number of lawsuits where celebrities have successfully stopped others from exploiting their personas. Among the notable cases, actors George Wendt and John Ratzenberger ("Norm" and "Cliff" from the sitcom *Cheers*) litigated to put the kibosh on a chain of taverns that had contracted with the sitcom's producers to place mannequin replicas of the *Cheers* characters in its bars. While there was no question that the producers owned the intellectual property rights to the characters they were licensing to the taverns, the lawsuit focused on whether or not what was being appropriated was the image of the *actors* who portrayed those characters. On that issue, the actors succeeded in court.[22]

It should be noted that the right of publicity doesn't extend only to appropriations of the actual likeness of a celebrity. Where an imitation is utilized to conjure that celebrity's persona, courts have also found that to be grounds for successful litigation. Game show hostess Vanna White sued to put a stop to a TV commercial that featured a robot outfitted to satirically resemble her. In ruling in her favor, the Ninth Circuit Court of Appeals said, "The right of publicity does not require that appropriations of identity be accomplished through particular means to be actionable."[23] In this case, a recognizable approximation of Ms. White was sufficient.

While cases such as this often involve public figures who possess highly marketable personas—the likes of which most of the rest of us don't have—that doesn't mean there are no protections for the likeness of the ordinary person. If you're out in public and a news photographer snaps your photo at a protest rally, you can't stop the newspaper from publishing that photograph—even if the revelation of your attendance at that rally might prove embarrassing for you. (Didn't you tell the boss you needed the day off to care for a sick child?) Freedom of the press rules in this situation, and you've neither a right to privacy in a public place nor a right to overrule the First Amendment. However, if someone were to start selling your photo on T-shirts without your consent, you could make a case against that person for the unauthorized commercial exploitation of your image.

It's absolutely amazing to me how many people—including people whom you'd think would know better—fail to grasp this concept. So let's take a moment to make this very clear.

What if you spot Denzel Washington buying a hot dog from a street vendor. You whip out your trusty camera and snap a photo of the actor as he chows down on the hot dog. Can you sell that photo to a newspaper even if you don't have the actor's permission to do so? Yes, you can. The public activities of celebrities are sometimes deemed to be news stories—albeit, often of the "tabloid" variety. You're free to sell the photo to the newspaper for whatever profit you can attain, and the newspaper is free to publish it. In this case, Mr. Washington has no say in the matter.

---

22 *Wendt v. Host International,* a case that twice went before the Ninth Circuit Court of Appeals.

23 *White v. Samsung Electronics America.*

But what if you decide you'd like to turn that same photo into a poster with the caption, "Denzel Goes to the Dogs"? Can you market that poster legally without Mr. Washington's permission? The answer is *no*. In this case, the purpose of the publication of the photo isn't for the reporting of a news event (something protected by the First Amendment) but, rather, for a commercial exploitation of another person's image. The marketability of the poster isn't merely derived from your talents as a photographer but, also, from the celebrity of its subject, Denzel Washington. That's what you're really cashing in on. A photograph of a non-celebrity eating a hot dog would be unlikely to have the same marketable appeal.

A right of publicity can sometimes be inherited by the heirs of a deceased person. Even though a person is dead, his family may still have the right to control the exploitation of his name and likeness for a certain period of time. What's more, because the right of publicity is viewed as a property right, it's a right that can be transferred to others, either by the subject while he's alive or by his heirs after he's gone. The rules vary by state. Some recognize a right of publicity by statute, others by case law. Some have not recognized it. If you're unsure whether the deceased person whose likeness you want to appropriate has an active right of publicity, consult a lawyer or research the current statutes or case law for the state where the person was residing when he died. That's likely to be the controlling law.

If you're worried about what law applies to the right of privacy for a deceased person—don't worry. The right of privacy doesn't extend beyond the grave. Once a person is gone, so is any right of privacy that person had.

Even non-celebrities have a right to control the use of their own likenesses. For this reason, artists who make use of the names or likenesses of real people often use *model releases* or *depiction releases* as a legal safeguard. Sure, you could always just ask someone, "Do you mind if I take your picture and put it in my art gallery?" and the person might just say, "Sure, go ahead." But then what are going to do later if the photo is the buzz of the art world, people are bidding the price up beyond anything you had ever imagined, and the person whose image is in that photo suddenly shows up at your doorstep to claim he never gave you permission to *sell* the photo?

A model release is typically unnecessary if no one person is truly the subject of the work. That is, if, for example, it's a photo of a crowd and no one is specifically identifiable in it, you shouldn't have to get a release signed from each and every person in the crowd in order to be able to utilize the photo. However, if you intend to commercially exploit someone's clearly identifiable likeness, it's a safer course of action to get a written release signed by that person. You might have to cut that person in for a piece of the action, but better to get that negotiated at the start rather than later when you're counting on being able to use the work, and the subject's lack of consent has you over a barrel.

A release doesn't have to be a lengthy document. It need be only as long as it takes to recite the rights you need it to cover. A one-page model release might be sufficient for a photographer whose limited purpose is just to be able to display, copy, and market a photo. In fact, brevity might be a benefit for the roving artist who's trying to capture candid glimpses of people he happens to run across. Present someone you don't know with a five-page release document, and that person might be disinclined to sign it. That's why it's important that a release for such situations state clearly, succinctly, and in plain language that non-lawyers can readily understand, what permissions the signer is granting to the artist. A very simple model release might look something like this:

ILLUSTRATION OF A SIMPLE MODEL RELEASE FORM

I, [model's name] , do hereby give to [artist's name] , as well as to his successors and assigns and any person or company acting with his permission, full right and permission to use my likeness, photograph(s), voice and/or name for advertising, publicity, commercial or non-commercial trade, or any other lawful purpose, in any medium now known or hereafter to be developed, and do hereby release, acquit and forever discharge [artist's name] , his successors and assigns, and anyone acting with his permission, from any and all claims, actions, causes of action, and liabilities arising out of any use of my likeness, photograph(s), voice, and/or name.

I am over 18 years of age.

Signature of model: _____

Date: _____

Do keep in mind that the above is merely an *illustration* of possible language for a model release. It does not address every contingency that a particular artist may require.

Among the other things to keep in mind when crafting a more detailed model release are:

- Does it state specifically what use will be made of the model's likeness and whether that use is for some particular purpose or all commercial purposes?
- Does it allow the artist to make unlimited reproductions or as many reproductions as the artist may require?
- Does it cover a particular medium or all media whether now known or hereafter devised?
- Does it allow for the artist to create derivative works?
- Does it state specifically that the model will hold the artist harmless (that is, not take any sort of legal action against the artist) for invasion of privacy or right of publicity, or hold the artist harmless if the model's likeness is somehow distorted or blurred in the finished work?
- Does it state that the rights are granted in perpetuity or for just a given period of time?
- Does it state that compensation or consideration will be provided to the model, and, if so, how will it be paid?

You'll recall from our discussion of contract law that a contract isn't valid without *consideration*—that is something of value that's exchanged to each party. When you're hiring a model, there's typically some monetary compensation involved for that person's services, and so there's no issue over consideration. However, if you're not hiring the person whose likeness you're appropriating, payment for the use of that person's likeness may never come into the picture. Does that present a problem for the artist? Well, if the primary purpose of the release is just to have the model state for the record that he won't sue for invasion of privacy if his likeness is published, then, unless you're in a state that has a different requirement, you probably don't need a consideration clause. All you're really asking for there is a written assurance that the model is okay with you using his likeness for some venture. However, if you want to shore up a model release where you're having doubts about your ability to make it stick, you might think about offering the subject something of value (perhaps his own copy of the finished work) as consideration.

Depiction releases for the subjects of movies, television programs, or other theatrical works, are likely to be more detailed than a simple model release. If, for example, you wish to purchase the exclusive rights to Margaret's life story so that you can make a film about her, the extent of the rights being granted needs to be decided and specified in the depiction release. Margaret may not be willing to sell you every conceivable privilege of exploiting her life story. She may want some restrictions. After all, it's *her life* we're talking about. So among the questions to be answered is whether the release is limited to just a film depiction of her story or whether it also includes such things as later remakes, sequels, prequels, adaptations for stage or television, radio rights, related merchandising, and book rights. Also to be answered is the question of whether you require Margaret's cooperation in the creation of the film and, if so, to what degree? Will you be needing access to personal papers, letters, diaries? Will you need to interview her? Will you need to interview and depict in the film other persons in her life, and, if so, will that necessitate getting releases from all of them, too?

Another thing that might be included in the release is whether you have the right to fictionalize portions of Margaret's story. A certain degree of literary license is very common in moviemaking, although not always appreciated by the subjects being depicted. Margaret might be a little leery of letting you tinker with her story. If she's a concert pianist, she might not fully appreciate how you've "improved" the story by redrafting the script to make her character a kazoo-playing street performer. Fearing that, she might want the depiction release to include a clause that allows for her to have script approval rights.

Be very, very cautious when negotiating approval rights in any project. If you give that right away to someone else, your project can be held at that person's mercy. Should an artistic standoff occur, your project could be brought to a complete halt. Rather than giving away script approval, a safer route might be to offer that all changes to the story will be made *in consultation* with Margaret, but that *you* will retain final script approval.

Additionally, since Margaret may not want to wait for the rest of her life for you to get around to making this movie, the release might also have some durational maximum in terms of a time limit (often known as an *option* period) in which you possess the exclusive right to exploit her story. Once the time period elapses, if you haven't exercised the option, all rights revert back to Margaret, and she's free to sell her life story to someone else.

Another thing to keep in mind about releases—and, for that matter, any signed legal instruments—minors cannot legally sign releases. If the subject is under the age of eighteen, the signature of a parent or legal guardian will be necessary on the release, and that release should specifically state that the parent or guardian is granting permission to utilize the child's name and/or likeness.

Fictional Characters

Okay, so enough with real people and all the real problems they can cause the artist who just wants to make something creative without ending up in court. Maybe you'll just stick to fictional characters. That'll be safe, won't it?

Well—and I know you're getting tired of this kind of response, but it's just the way the law works—it depends. Are you creating an original character with unique characteristics derived out of your own fertile mind? Or are you borrowing elements of someone else's character—elements that people would recognize as unique to that other character? If it's the latter, you could run into legal complications. To help you avoid those complications, let's talk a little about what's fair game among fictional characters and what isn't.

First, as we noted earlier, characters are generally not copyrightable. You can't concoct a story about a hardboiled detective who solves sinister crimes and claim you've now got a lock on all similar detective characters. Allowing such a monopoly on so general an archetype would seriously cramp the creative output of the mystery genre—something that would run counter to copyright's mission to enrich the world by *promoting* creativity. So, if you create such a character for your own work, you ought to be free and clear of any legal hassles so far as copyright laws are concerned. However, copyright can play a protective role where the pictorial representations and verbal descriptions are not a mere delineation of character traits but, rather, go beyond the general and into the realm of a specific arrangement of incidents and literary expressions that set a particular character apart from all others. That is, where a character is so distinctly etched into the public's mind that a near twin would cause people to say, "Oh, that's just *Character X* with a different name," it can be possible to copyright that character and preclude imitators from cashing in on the well known character's fame.

"Copyright a character?! Who among us," you ask, "is capable of such marvels?!"

Well, my friends...who else?

Faster than a speeding subpoena...
More powerful than a writ of habeas corpus...
Able to leap tall dockets in a single bound...

Yes, it's *Superman*. Strange visitor from another planet who fights a never ending battle for truth, justice, and the American way of getting all over the case of anybody who comes anywhere near infringing his intellectual property. Superman is a prime example of a character that has been copyrighted. He has a specific look, a specific costume, and some extremely specific powers that aren't your run-of-the-mill, garden-variety character traits. There's just no mistaking Superman, and the owners of the Superman copyright have stood a decades-long vigil to guard against what they've viewed as wannabe copycat superheroes.

In the 1940 case, *Detective Comics v. Bruns Publications*, the company that controlled the rights to Superman went head to head with the company that produced a competing comic book superhero called Wonderman, which the Superman people claimed infringed their copyright in their character. In analyzing the case, the Second Circuit Court of Appeals compared the totality of traits in the two characters: each concealed his real identity and strength until needed; each used his powers to help the oppressed; each crushed guns in his bare hands; each could stop a fired bullet; each could leap over tall buildings; each was strong enough to bend steel; and each battled evil and injustice in the world. The biggest difference the court was able to note between the characters was that Superman wore a blue, skin-tight costume and Wonderman wore a red one. This fashion option was deemed insufficient by the court, which ruled that the creators of Wonderman "used more than general types and ideas and have appropriated the pictorial and literary details embodied in [Superman's] copyrights." While the court added that the people who owned the Superman franchise weren't entitled to monopolize any and all "super" characters, it did say that they had the right to prosecute for copyright infringement the creators of any character that embodied too similarly the particular visual and verbal representations of their "Superman." To put it simply, the more specific a character's look and traits, the stronger is the case for copyright protection of that character. This is why Superman and other cartoon characters have a better chance of being copyrightable than characters whose appearance is merely described in words or portrayed by actors. When a character is drawn, its exact look is cemented in the public's mind and is not subject to the varying appearances of actors who might play the character in film/TV productions, or subject to the differences of opinion that might occur in the public's mind if it's left to imagine, from a verbal or written description, what the character looks like. From his earliest comic book days, there's been no mistaking the appearance of Superman or his specific super abilities.

Now, lest you think this makes Superman absolutely unbeatable when going up against similar superheroes, I call your attention to a case that, like kryptonite, stopped Superman in his tracks when he tried to pull the plug on a TV show titled *The Greatest American Hero*. The short-lived program was about the exploits of an ordinary milquetoast who becomes a superhero *à la* the Superman motif. As a super crime fighter, the hero of the show was of a bumbling, humorous variety, typically saving the day almost in spite of himself. However, there was no mistaking the similarities of his powers to those of Superman, and anyone watching *The Greatest American Hero* would repeatedly be reminded of the iconic cartoon hero long established in comics, movies, and television. The Superman owners sued, claiming the new show's superhero infringed their copyright.

Once again it was the Second Circuit Court of Appeals that heard the case[24] and, this time, ruled in favor of the defendants who produced *The Greatest American Hero* TV show. "Stirring one's memory of a copyrighted character," wrote the court, "is not the same as appearing to be substantially similar to that character, and only the latter is infringement." The court examined the similarities and the differences between the characters, and, while it was careful to say that it's not necessary that every single character trait be an exact duplicate to constitute copyright infringement, "the total perception of all ideas as expressed in each character" was a concluding factor in its decision that the two characters were fundamentally different. *The Greatest American Hero* had not infringed on the Man of Steel. (Sorry, big guy. Ya can't win 'em all.)

Keep in mind that you can parody a character, even if it's copyrighted. That's a fair use. Even Superman's not impervious to parody.

Also keep in mind that, while a character itself can't be trademarked, it can *become* the trademark of a merchandising venture. When that happens,

---

24 *Warner Brothers v. American Broadcasting Companies.*

be especially careful about any appropriations of similar character traits. Bugs Bunny and Mickey Mouse have their images on more products than you'd want to sit and count. If you plaster a substantially similar rabbit or rodent image on merchandise of your own, it could confuse the public into thinking the source of that merchandise is Warner Brothers or Disney, and, as we know, trademark law's whole purpose is to avoid confusion.

Oh, and if you do infringe on a Warner Brothers or Disney trademark… you can expect their lawyers to be on you faster than a speeding bullet.

Music Rights

Probably nowhere is there a greater misunderstanding or more blatant abuse of intellectual property than that which occurs in regard to music rights. Either people don't think there's a copyright involved in music; or they don't think it applies to what they're doing; or the very notion of property rights never even enters their heads when they're doing something with someone else's song. You might think that people in the performing arts would at least be cognizant of musical copyrights and the restrictions that guard against unauthorized utilization of music. However, it has been my longtime observation that the same artist who wouldn't sit still for someone else making an unauthorized appropriation of a portion of that artist's play or dance or film has no qualms whatsoever about plopping someone else's copyright-protected song into his own work without giving the slightest thought that there might be anyone whose permission needs to be requested.

Yes, music's all around us. It's broadcast on radio and TV, playing in the background of restaurants and bars, streaming on the web, digitized on our iPods, concertized in halls and theaters, and performed by people on the streets and in the subways for the coins passersby might throw. And perhaps it's this ubiquitous nature of music that relegates to an afterthought—if, indeed, it's even thought of at all—that there are people who composed the notes, wrote the lyrics, produced the performance, and created the recordings. These things didn't just fall out of heaven and land on your eardrums. Somebody actually *owns* those songs. They're not wildflowers freely available for the picking.

First, there's a copyright that belongs to whoever wrote the song. Composers and lyricists all have a legitimate claim for copyright protection since they, like any other artist creating an original work, have fixed their artistic expression in the form of a written piece of sheet music. When you buy sheet music, part of the price reflects the royalty paid to those who created the song. As artists, most if not all of us can appreciate the fairness of sharing the economic proceeds of music sales with those who are its original creators. Hey, if it weren't for those people, there would be no song. Oftentimes, they will sell the song's copyright to a music publisher, but that's just a transfer of the rights, not a disintegration of them. Whether the rights are held by the original creators or by someone else to whom they've been assigned, you can assume most contemporary music is copyrighted, and any public use of that music needs to be authorized by the copyright holder.

Second, if the music has been recorded, there's a second copyright—this one a copyright on the recording itself. A recording is a derivative work of the original composition, and, typically, the copyright on the recording is held by the record label. Since there are two separate copyrights in play for a recorded piece of music, someone wishing to utilize the recording for some public purpose needs to secure the permission of *both* copyright holders—the one who holds the copyright to the music and the one who holds the copyright to the recording. You can't simply get authorization from the record label and assume you've got carte blanche permission to utilize that recording in any way you see fit. Remember the case where the underlying play in the movie version of *Pygmalion* was separately protected, even after the copyright in the film adaptation of it was allowed to lapse? It works the same way here. The composition that is the underlying work of the recording doesn't give up its own separate copyright just because it has been adapted into a derivative recorded work.[25]

It should be noted that an old song, like all other creative works, will eventually fall into the public domain. The majority of classical music, for instance, was written pre-1923. You won't have to look up any of Mozart's descendents to ask if you can play *Eine Kleine Nachtmusik* in your theater company's production of *Amadeus*. However, if you want to include the London Philharmonic recording of it as part of the show, you'll need to ask permission of the recording's copyright holder.

Also take note that the duration of the copyright on a recording is timed from the date that particular recording was created and distributed, not from some past date the artist may have first recorded it. To clarify, there

---

25 It's possible that the publisher and the recording label could be one and the same and, therefore, possibly control the copyrights for both the composition and the recording. However, one should never assume that without checking.

are some very old recordings archived practically from the days of Thomas Edison's first phonograph. While those original recordings may date back a hundred years or more, if they're re-issued in a newly mastered recording put out today, that means there's a brand new copyright on that particular, new recording, and it will stay in effect for the full duration under current copyright laws.[26]

Whether you're talking about the right to use the composition, a recording of it, or both in some sort of public performance[27], one of two types of rights apply: *small performing rights* or *grand rights*. To determine whose permission is needed, it's necessary to determine which of these performing rights you require.

Non-dramatic uses of music fall within the scope of *small performing rights*, which is, generally speaking, the rights regarding any public performance of a song that's not playing an integral part in an overall, contextual work. In other words, this could include the playing of background music in such venues as a restaurant, a bar, or a store, or it could be a more prominently featured performance of the music at a concert or on the radio. Such performances are typically categorized as non-dramatic because there's no particular storyline linking the songs together. Rather, in this sort of musical presentation, songs are performed either individually or in a cabaret-style revue that isn't connected to any plot. For performances of this ilk, a small performing rights license is what you need.

The small performing rights for most published songs in this country are managed by one of three performing rights societies: the American Society of Composers, Authors and Publishers (better known as ASCAP),

---

26   Just in case you're still a little unclear on this—an example: It's been quite a while since opera sensation Enrico Caruso recorded any music. He died in 1921. Yet there are still recordings of Mr. Caruso in existence, and you can buy them from the standard music outlets. However, if you buy a Caruso album from one of those outlets, you can bet they're not going to go fishing in some moldy chamber and dust off a wax disk that was manufactured around the beginning of the 20th century. Rather, they're going to pull out a recording that was re-mastered from the original sometime in the not-too-distant past when modern sound recording equipment allowed for a quality reproduction that's compatible with present-day sound systems. It's the date of that new re-mastering that counts as the creation date of that recording, not the date when Mr. Caruso first sang the song into a microphone.

27   Section 101 of the Copyright Act defines a public performance as one that is "open to the public or at any place where a substantial number of persons outside of a normal circle of a family and its social acquaintances is gathered."

Broadcast Music, Inc. (better known as BMI), and SESAC (which its website says "for history's sake" originally stood for Society of European Stage Authors and Composers). Each organization controls the issuance of small performing rights licenses for the music in its catalogue. A blanket license for a society's entire catalogue can be secured by anyone, and, if you buy blanket licenses from all three, you have the luxury of playing just about any published song in existence in a non-dramatic format.[28]

The legal responsibility for purchasing the license falls on the shoulders of the producer, typically whoever manages the venue where the music will be played. For example, let's say Marc operates what's known as a "cover band"—that is, it's a band that performs music that was written by someone other than Marc or the members of his band. Should the band get a gig playing at the Jolly Good Times Saloon, it won't be Marc's responsibility to secure small performing rights licenses from ASCAP, BMI, and SESAC. That will be up to Jolly Good Times Saloon. If Jolly Good Times makes a regular practice of hiring cover bands, then it will probably be to the saloon's benefit to negotiate annual licenses from the societies so that the venue will be properly licensed no matter which band is playing there.

Naturally, licenses are only necessary if the music being played is controlled by one or more of the societies. If Marc's band plays only music its members composed themselves, then, assuming they haven't sold the performance rights of those songs to someone else, no license would be needed. Additionally, if all of the music to be played is controlled by only one of the societies, then a license from just that one society would suffice. However, for safety's sake, venues that feature live music will often purchase licenses from all three societies so that they don't accidentally run afoul of the law if one of the bands suddenly does a song that's not in the catalogue of a society with which they have a licensing agreement.

Small performing rights licenses need to be purchased in advance of a performance. It's not a "pay as you play" kind of business.

Now let's look at another situation. Let's say Nancy runs a theater company. Before the show and during intermission, she plays recorded music in

---

28   The contact information for general licensing at the three societies is:
       ASCAP, 2675 Paces Ferry Road, SE, Suite 350, Atlanta, GA 30339; (800) 505-4052; ascap.com
       BMI, 320 West 57th St., New York, NY 10019; (888) 689-5264; bmi.com
       SESAC, 5 Music Square East, Nashville, TN 37203; (615) 320-0055; sesac.com

the theater. Such use of copyright protected recordings would be covered by a small performing rights license. Yes, even though the music isn't part of the show itself, and even though it's just background sound that's not having any special attention called to it, a license is still required to legally play the recordings where her audience can hear it. That's considered a public performance.

But what happens if the play at Nancy's theater has a scene where that very same music is sung or danced to by one of the characters in the show? Well, here now we've gone beyond a non-dramatic performance of the music and into something that's incorporating the music as an integral part of the play's story. That's a dramatic use of song, and it's no longer covered by a small performing rights license. For this you need a *grand rights* license. Grand rights are also sometimes referred to as "dramatic performing rights" because a song that's put into a dramatic performance assumes a theatrical purpose when it's an element of the plot or theme.

ASCAP, BMI, and SESAC don't control grand rights. Those rights are typically withheld by the song's composer or publisher, and that's whose permission has to be secured to put a copyright-protected song into a drama.

But now what if Nancy decides to have the music played in the background during the play's performance, just to help set the mood of the scene? No singing. No dancing. No one on stage even references the song. Just a little touch of musical ambiance. Does a small performing rights license cover that?

The answer is *no*. That still requires a grand rights license. This is a highly misunderstood component of copyright law, and one that I suspect is subjected to frequent and routine infringement at the hands of people who don't even realize they're doing anything illegal. Even just as background music, if a song is being played as part of a scene, it's being used in a dramatic sense. That makes it a part of the dramatic story. That's a very different situation from a restaurant playing recorded music in the background of its dining room where there is no dramatic performance taking place.

I shudder at the thought of rampant copyright infringement taking place in theaters round the world every time a playwright or a director says, "Ya know what'd be good in this scene?—a song!" But you sense that it must be happening all the time—especially in smaller companies where you just get the feeling that nobody's in charge of securing and paying for performance rights to music.

For the record, this sort of thing isn't restricted only to plays that incorporate music. It also applies to ballet, opera, film, broadcast media, or any other work of art or entertainment that tells a dramatic story. If you decide to incorporate someone else's copyright protected music into a dramatic performance, a grand rights license from the copyright holder is required. Additionally, when music is added to any media involving recorded visual images (such as film, TV, computer programs and games, and other audiovisual formats), a separate *synchronization license* must also be secured from the publisher. And then there's the *mechanical license* that must be attained if you're distributing recorded copies of something that includes a recording of a song you don't own.[29]

I know this truly galls some people who consider it a major imposition on their creative talents to have to jump through such legal hoops and pay for various licenses simply to stay within the law. But I ask you to keep in mind that copyright is a two-edged sword. As anxious as you are to protect your own intellectual property from misappropriation (and every artist I've ever known has been keenly anxious to do that), others who possess marketable artistic creations, such as music, are just as anxious to protect their works.

Okay, so while you chew on that bit of philosophy, let's go back to Marc's band, and let's say the band has landed a recording contract. It's going to cut an album—or, as the United States Copyright Office likes to call it, a *phonorecord*. Being a cover band with no original music of its own, does Marc's band have to ask permission and negotiate a non-dramatic, small rights performing license with each and every publisher of every song it's going to record?

You may actually like the answer to this one. The answer is *no*. Under Section 115 of the Copyright Act, once a phonorecord of a musical work has been publicly distributed in this country with the copyright owner's consent, anyone else is then free to make and distribute phonorecords of their own version of that same song *without* the express permission of the copyright owner. This is what's known as *compulsory license*.

The way it works is this: Let's say Marc wants his band to record their rendition of the Elton John song, *Bennie and the Jets*. The first thing Marc

---

29   The foremost agency for mechanical licensing in America is the Harry Fox Agency, Inc., located at 601 West 26th St., Suite 500, New York, NY 10001; (212) 834-0100; harryfox.com.

needs to do is to identify the song's copyright owner (something he might be able to do by searching the Copyright Office records). Then, sometime within thirty days after making the recording (and before any distribution of it occurs), he would serve by certified or registered mail a *Notice of Intention to Obtain a Compulsory License* on that copyright owner. (It doesn't need to be filed with the Copyright Office.) Once distribution of the phonorecord begins, Marc needs to file with the copyright owner a detailed Annual Statement of Account that's certified by a certified public accountant, and he needs to make statutory royalty payments[30] accompanied by a Monthly Statement of Account to the copyright owner.

Note that nowhere in the above instructions does it say anything about the copyright owner having to give consent or the copyright owner having the right to forbid the recording of the song. Such rights simply don't apply in this case. That's why it's a *compulsory* license. So long as Marc plays within the rules, his band is free to make all the records they like, regardless of whether Elton John or anyone else thinks Marc's rendition of the song is any good. What's more, Marc can make a new musical arrangement of the song without running afoul of copyright law. However, it should be noted that a new arrangement under a compulsory license does *not* automatically constitute a derivative of the original song, and that new arrangement probably can't be protected by a separate copyright.

Just so you know, if the name and address of the copyright owner of the song can't be found, you still have to file a Notice of Intention to Obtain a Compulsory License, only in this case it's filed with the Copyright Office along with a statutory fee. To be entitled to receive royalties under a compulsory license, the copyright owner must be identified in the Copyright Office's records. Once identified, the copyright owner is entitled to royalties on every compulsory license phonorecord made from that time forward, but he's not entitled to recover royalties for any previously made and distributed phonorecords.

Now just so we're clear on this...The Copyright Act defines "phonorecords" as "material objects in which sounds, other than those accompanying a motion picture or other audiovisual work are fixed." That means movie/TV soundtracks are not eligible for a compulsory license, but music CDs, tapes,

---

30 The statutory royalties are determined by the Copyright Arbitration Royalty Panels. Those royalties are based on a *per phonorecord* rate. Check with the Copyright Office for the current rate.

and digital recordings (whether distributed in the form of a tangible medium or by digital download) are eligible. Furthermore, a compulsory license is exclusively for the *distribution* of music to the public for *private use*, which means background music systems, jukeboxes, broadcasting, and other *public* uses are not eligible for compulsory license.

One last thing about music rights...YouTube and other websites are not magical lands immune to the laws of copyright. Although, based on the kinds of things that sometimes get uploaded to such sites, it would be hard to make a convincing argument that there isn't a large group of people who are under the impression that copyright just doesn't apply to the Internet. Let me assure you that it does. That means your incorporation of a Billie Holiday recording as background music for your film about New York street scenes, or the home video of your eight-year-old daughter lip-syncing to Cher's recording of "If I Could Turn Back Time," are both governed by the above rules when you put them on the Internet for the world to see and hear. The Internet is a form of publishing, and republishing someone's copyright-protected music requires permission. Yes, much of this type of thing goes on without incident or challenge, either because it goes principally unnoticed or because there's a general indifference on the part of the copyright owners. But that doesn't mean it's legal. And a word to the wise: What your daughter might get away with when she's publishing online only for the amusement of her friends, and what you might get away with when you cyber-publish a work of art that gains significant attention and notoriety, could be two entirely different things.

What Is the Artist Allowed and Not Allowed to Say?

From almost the beginning we've been saying that the laws governing intellectual property apply to fixed expressions of ideas. An *expression*, by its very nature, is a form of *communication*, regardless of whether it's embodied in words, sounds, images, or actions. Therefore, when we're talking about an artist's expression, we're talking about the artist conveying *meaning* to others through whichever medium is utilized to create the art. That meaning may be serious, silly, profound, whimsical, political, sensual, or any of the other thought-provoking or emotion-inducing possibilities that can result when someone encounters and experiences another's expression of ideas. Even a painting depicting a group of dogs playing poker is a creative expression that—while it may be unlikely it'll ever be displayed in the Museum of Modern Art—still conveys some meaning, albeit in an extremely light-hearted, farcical fashion. A poem, a book, a movie, a song, a dance, a play, a sculpture, a sketch, a photo, a painting—even one of those poker-playing dogs—or any other artistic creation you can think of is the tangible form by which the artist speaks to the world. And here in the United States of America we enjoy what's arguably the greatest freedom of speech the world knows. Hats off to the original framers of our federal government who thought to tack on a First Amendment to the Constitution.

The bountiful graces of our freedom of speech notwithstanding, there are a few rules and restrictions by which speech in America is governed or curtailed. For example—and this example probably goes without saying—you're not legally permitted to falsely yell "Fire!" in a crowded theater where such a yell could cause needless panic resulting in injuries, disturbance, or emotional distress. That's not the sort of speech the First Amendment was designed to protect.

In this chapter, we'll examine the rights and restrictions associated with speech and how they might apply to artists working in any genre or medium. Our freedoms in this regard far outnumber our restrictions. So, for our purposes, this doesn't need to be a lengthy examination. But what rights and restrictions there are that relate to speech in America are important enough for us to take note.

First Amendment Protections

> *Congress shall make no law...abridging the freedom of speech...*

With those simple words, incorporated into the United States Constitution—a document that is the supreme law of the land—Americans have enjoyed the right to speak their minds, rightly or wrongly, popularly or unpopularly, for more than two centuries. We take it for granted that this is a birthright, which, under our law, it is. Without this provision of the First Amendment, government might be able to silence those with whom it disagreed, and one might only imagine the added difficulties that once controversial movements led by the likes of Susan B. Anthony, Cesar Chavez, and Martin Luther King, Jr., might have encountered were it not for the legal protections safeguarding their right to publicly bring their causes to light.

Born of a revolution spurred by, among other things, the grievance that American colonists didn't have a representative voice in the foreign government that once ruled the land, the United States has long held dear the notion that political speech should enjoy the maximum freedom it can be afforded. If you're making a political statement with your art, you have the full force of the United States Constitution behind you. However, as I said a little while ago, even then there are some restrictions. You can't club someone over the head with your clay sculpture and call it a political statement. (Okay, I suppose you could *call* it that, but you'd still go to jail for assault and battery. So I highly recommend you not effect your political speech through acts of violence.)

Controversial, and even objectionable, speech is protected by the First Amendment.[31] Such speech needs to be protected, or all minority viewpoints would be at risk of being squelched by a majority with a different opinion. Our Bill of Rights (the first ten amendments to the Constitution) is not about the rights of a majority of citizens. It's about the rights of each *individual*, and, as we've all heard recited before, you've got to guarantee to your worst enemy the same right that you, yourself, claim as your own. Deny your enemy a right today, and tomorrow that same right will be denied to you should you need to exercise it.

So how does this apply to you as an artist? It means that, even when you create art that causes someone else to be offended, outraged, or shocked by its content, it is *protected speech* in this country. Even if there's no one else on the planet besides you who isn't appalled by what you've created, it's still a protected expression.

The same holds true for highly critical speech. Just like parody, which we discussed in the last chapter, art that comments either directly or indirectly on a person or entity in the public eye, whether that comment is complimentary or critical, is art that's making the kind of fair comment and criticism that encourages public discourse on the issues of the day. That's precisely the sort of thing the framers were trying to promote when they drafted such wide open language about freedom of speech in the First Amendment. The thinking back then was that only through allowing the grandest scope of information to gain public access would the populace be able to weigh all the elements of the available opinions and draw its own educated, well-reasoned conclusions.

Getting back to our example of yelling "Fire!" in a crowded theater... the doctrine of free speech shouldn't be confused with a policy of "anything goes." Government is allowed to create some standards where public safety and security are concerned. However, government can't impose prior restrictions on the content of speech unless the government can meet what's called a *strict scrutiny* standard.

Strict scrutiny is the highest standard by which government needs to make its case for taking some action. Not everything government does is compelled to meet such a standard. Examples of things that trigger the

---

31   Past court rulings have included such things as flag burning, cross burning, and painted swastikas as forms of protected speech.

strict scrutiny test are laws involving the right to marry or have children, the right to travel freely, the right to vote, the free exercise of religion, and free speech. If government attempts to regulate any of these things, the strict scrutiny standard requires the government to show that the law is necessary to achieve a *compelling government purpose*. That is, the objective of the law must be vital and necessary, and it must be shown that there is no less restrictive alternative that will achieve the objective.

To illustrate this, let's say Priscilla is opening a photo exhibition titled "The Art of Love," which features images of people in various stages of undress who are engaged in love-making activities. Artistic though the composition of these photos may be, the content is the sort of thing that might be deemed inappropriate for small children. Government could argue that it has a compelling interest in protecting the very young from accidentally encountering things of a sexual nature that are geared toward a more mature audience, and, based on that, the local government could take action. However, if the city council voted to shut down Priscilla's exhibition altogether, one would have to ask, under the strict scrutiny standard, if there wasn't a less restrictive alternative to a total shutdown. The obvious alternative that springs to mind would be to require a minimum age for admission to the photo exhibition. That would serve the purpose of achieving the government's interest in protecting the children of its community, but in a way that doesn't totally infringe Priscilla's right to freedom of speech. In this case, if it went to court, a law closing the exhibit entirely would stand a good chance of being struck down as unconstitutional, while a law requiring a minimum age might be deemed appropriate and legal.

Restrictions on Free Speech

In the interest of maintaining order, government has always had the privilege of imposing rules regarding the time, place, and manner by which speech may be publicly exercised.

If, for example, Joe wishes to voice his displeasure with a decision made by the local school board, and his method of doing this is by staging a satirical demonstration in the form of street theater that ridicules the board's decision, Joe is certainly free to stage the performance where members of the public can view it. However, if he decides that the best place to hold the performance is on the sidewalk just outside the windows of a school classroom while class is in session, the noise and distracting nature of Joe's performance could create a situation where the students in the classroom aren't able to concentrate and learn their lessons. As education is an important government purpose, government has the right to restrict speech that threatens that purpose. In this case, while the government has no right to forbid Joe's demonstration on a public street, it could require him to take it someplace out of earshot of the classrooms, or, in the alternative, require that he conduct the performance outside the school only at times when classes aren't in session.

The key to a time, place, and manner restriction on speech in a public forum such as a sidewalk or a park is that the restriction must be narrowly tailored, allow for some adequate alternative to what is being restricted, and it must be *subject matter and viewpoint neutral.* By "subject matter and viewpoint neutral," I mean that the government can't legally deny Joe the ability to stage his critical performance outside the school while also allowing someone else to stage a demonstration complimentary of the school board in the same place and at a similar time. That sort of government-sanctioned favoritism based on content would be unconstitutional.

We talk about government-funded facilities as "public property." However, simply because the government owns or operates a space, that doesn't necessarily mean that the space is automatically an open public forum where unfettered speech is permitted. Military installations and prisons would be just two examples of facilities where the government is not required to permit access for the exercise of free speech. The government may regulate speech in such non-public forums where such regulations are deemed to be reasonable and where there is a *legitimate* (as opposed to important) government interest. On those occasions where the government would be allowed to close a forum to public speech but, instead, chooses to open it, then the same rules apply as those for public forums regarding how the government may impose time, place, and manner restrictions.

To be absolutely clear about this, so far we've been talking about First Amendment restrictions on the *government.* The Amendment specifically states that the United States Congress shall make no laws abridging the freedom of speech, and that restriction has also been applied to state governments through the Fourteenth Amendment. But nowhere does it say private citizens can't limit what's said on their own property. *There's no First Amendment right to use someone else's private property for the exercise of free speech.* Should an artist named Debbi decide she'd like to paint a politically themed mural on the side of a privately owned building, she first needs to get the permission of the building's owner. If you come along later and ask that same owner for permission to paint another wall of the building with a mural expressing a viewpoint that differs from Debbi's, that building's owner is under no obligation to grant that permission to you. On their own property, owners can be as *un*neutral about subject matter and viewpoint as they like. That's *their* First Amendment right.[32]

Despite the broad protections our speech is guaranteed, there are some forms of speech that can be absolutely outlawed and punished. Among those forms is what's sometimes referred to as *incendiary speech*. The government may punish someone whose speech is purposely trying to cause a substantial likelihood of some imminent illegality. It's all perfectly legal to rouse a crowd with highly motivational, even angry words. However, if you rile up an angry mob to extreme hostility and then tell them to burn down city hall—such that there's a good chance they'll actually do it—that's not protected by the First Amendment.

Similarly unprotected is deceptive advertising. Commercial speech, generally, has its own protections, although not as strictly guarded by the First Amendment as is non-commercial or political speech. However, even if the statements in advertisements are technically true, if they carry an inherent risk of deceiving the public, they can be prohibited. That's the basis of false advertising laws.

Profane and indecent material—terms and acts that, despite varying personal definitions, we all understand on some level as being somewhere beyond the usual bounds of polite society—are generally protected forms of speech, as is sexually oriented content. There are, of course, certain

---

32   There's a controversial U.S. Supreme Court ruling in the 1980 case of *Pruneyard Shopping Center v. Robins*, where the Court held that the California state constitution could legally allow the state to require that the owners of a shopping mall permit the expression of free speech on their private retail property. Among the things the Court reasoned was that the owners had invited the public into the mall to come and go as they pleased, and there was little chance that anyone would associate the views of people expressing themselves in the shopping center with those of the owners. Additionally, the mall owners were at liberty to post signs or the like disavowing any connection with those exercising their own free speech inside the mall. In this case, free speech won out over free enterprise. As I said, this was a controversial decision and one that various states have attempted to narrow as they have felt they're allowed. Before deciding to express your views publicly in a privately owned retail establishment, it may be advisable first to check the laws of that jurisdiction.

restrictions imposed on this type of material. For example, local governments often use zoning and other ordinances to regulate the location and availability of such things as nude dancing and pornography in their communities, and federal law prohibits sending lewd and lascivious material through the U.S. mail.[33] The restrictions can become much greater when the material is deemed to be *obscene*. Obscenity, by virtue of its lacking any artistically, scientifically, or politically redeeming value, sheds almost all First Amendment protections.

Perhaps the most notable restrictions on such speech have been applied to the broadcast media. American broadcasting has come a long way since the days when television was bleeping suggestive phrasing on *The Smothers Brothers*. But there are still some lines that broadcasters don't cross, lest they incite the ire of the Federal Communications Commission with its power to levy fines. The FCC has defined "profanity as including language so grossly offensive to members of the public who actually hear it as to amount to a nuisance," and it has defined "indecency as language or material that, in context, depicts or describes, in terms patently offensive as measured by contemporary community standards for the broadcast medium, sexual or excretory organs or activities."[34] As a public safeguard, the FCC imposes time restrictions on when profane or indecent material may be broadcast over the airwaves.

The boundaries of the FCC's powers were tested in the 1970s when a radio station broadcast in the middle of an afternoon an unedited recording of George Carlin's famous monologue about the seven "filthy words" one could never say over the airwaves. As those who are familiar with the comedian's work know, Mr. Carlin said all seven in the bit and unabashedly repeated them in various colloquial phrases. The radio station had given a warning at the beginning that the language it was about to broadcast might be considered offensive to some listeners. However, a man who was listening to the radio with his young son tuned in after the warning, was offended by what he and his son heard, and complained to the FCC. Although the FCC's only action was to rule that the station could be subjected to administrative sanctions—sanctions that the FCC chose not to impose in this instance—the station's ownership challenged the FCC's ruling, claiming that the

---

33   18 U.S.C. § 1461.

34   These definitions are taken from the FCC website at www.fcc.gov/cgb/consumerfacts/obscene.html.

monologue might have been *indecent*, but it wasn't *obscene*, and, therefore, the station maintained that constitutional protections placed it beyond the agency's power to restrict its broadcast. The issue went all the way to the United States Supreme Court in a case known as *Federal Communications Commission v. Pacifica Foundation*. In a narrowly decided ruling (five of the nine justices supported it), the High Court upheld the FCC's right to regulate the broadcast of indecent material even when it isn't deemed to be obscene. In this instance, the public interest in protecting the ears of small children outweighed the public interest in unfettered speech.

It should be noted that the *Pacifica* Court didn't condemn Mr. Carlin's list of words to the Land of the Eternally Forbidden. In the Court's published opinion, Justice John Paul Stevens wrote, "Although these words ordinarily lack literary, political, or scientific value, they are not entirely outside the protection of the First Amendment. Some uses of even the most offensive words are unquestionably protected." As is so often the case when it comes to application of the law, context is an important factor.

As I said earlier, just about all First Amendment protections disappear when the content dips into the realm of what the law defines as obscene. The difficulty, of course, is in knowing exactly where to draw the line between indecency and obscenity. Over the years, the Supreme Court has offered some guidance in the form of a three-prong test. Content is deemed to be obscene if:

1. An average person, applying contemporary community standards, would find that the material, as a whole, appeals to the prurient interest;

2. The material is patently offensive under the applicable law prohibiting obscenity; and

3. Taken as a whole, the material lacks serious redeeming artistic, literary, political, or scientific value.[35]

Unfortunately, this test leaves us with yet another inexact term to define. I'm referring to the phrase, "contemporary community standards." What exactly are any given community's contemporary standards regarding obscenity? And, for that matter, who qualifies as an "average person" applying those standards? Would it be you? Me? My mother? We might all have very

---

35　The U.S. Supreme Court articulated this test in 1973 in the case of *Miller v. California*.

different opinions on this, even if we lived in the same community. It was this kind of imprecision that led Supreme Court Justice Potter Stewart to write in his concurring opinion for the case of *Jacobellis v. Ohio* that, while he couldn't specifically define obscenity, he concluded that "I know it when I see it."

Now I realize that, once again, I've let down those of you who were hoping for a bright-line, letter-of-the-law rule that you could live by with absolute assurance. But I'm afraid there just isn't any such thing when we're talking about a legal definition of obscenity.

Defamation

Let's create a hypothetical situation...

We'll say that Mary is writing a book about an actual person's experiences, and one of the chapters describes the horrible dinners that person used to have at his friend Earl's house. According to the stories Mary has heard, Earl's cooking made people sick every time he had a dinner party. Although Mary doesn't know Earl personally and has no first-hand experience attending any of Earl's dinners, she considers the stories about his atrocious cooking to be very comical and highly entertaining, and so she includes them in her book.

Entertaining though the stories may be, Mary could be traipsing into potentially dangerous territory. Unlike a parody, where everyone understands that the parody is simply a comic exaggeration utilized to make a fair comment and criticism, Mary's book is making certain *factual* assertions about Earl that readers would be led to believe are actually true, and Earl might not take too kindly to seeing such things in print. What if, for example, Earl happens to be a professional chef? While everyone's entitled to make fair comment on the quality of someone else's work (there's no such thing as a false *opinion*), Mary's statement about people getting "sick every time he had a dinner party" could besmirch Earl's professional reputation, and, even if the restaurant where he works has never had any incidents of food poisoning, the negative publicity about Earl could have such a seriously detrimental effect on business as to cost Earl his job. If the stories about Earl are true, then maybe he deserves the boot. But, if they're not true, then Mary's publication of such stories would cause Earl undeserved injury to his reputation and could give him grounds to sue her for *defamation*.

Defamation occurs when a false statement causes injury to a person's reputation or exposes that person to hatred, contempt, or ridicule, or it subjects that person to a loss of the good will and confidence others had for that person. As already noted, merely expressing a negative opinion about someone is not defamation so long as it's clear to the audience that what's being shared is an *opinion*. You get into a risky gray area when opinion is presented in such a way that people might mistake it for a fact that has been verified. For example...

> *"Earl's cooking tastes so bad, it makes me sick just thinking about it."*

...is quite obviously an opinion couched in a common, idiomatic phrase that would never be taken literally. Everyone knows that no one actually gets physically ill just from thinking about someone else's cooking. It's just an expression, similar to when someone says something like "The team's owner is blackmailing the city into building a new stadium." That's just rhetorical hyperbole. No one believes for a moment that the team's owner is actually committing the felony of criminal extortion. So there's no legitimate cause for a defamation action over a statement like that. However...

> *"Earl's cooking has caused those who've eaten it to become sick."*

...sounds more like a statement of fact that's derived from conclusive evidence. If you don't actually have such evidence, and you don't mean for it to be taken literally, publishing that second statement is practically the legal equivalent of juggling dynamite. It could blow up on you at any time. If Earl loses his job because you made people believe his food gave his customers food poisoning—which it really didn't—you're going to have a hard time explaining to the judge why you uttered such an unjustifiable slander.

There are two basic branches of defamation: *slander*, which involves the spoken word; and *libel*, which involves printed or broadcast communications. Perhaps the biggest difference between them is that, with libel, the plaintiff doesn't need to prove damages to take his case before a jury. With some slander, he does need to prove damages. Beyond that, there's little to no significant difference between them for our purposes here. So we'll simply refer to both slander and libel collectively as defamation.

Some jurisdictions also recognize a separate action known as *false light* where someone portrays another in a false or misleading sense that would be highly offensive or embarrassing to a reasonable person. False light could include such things as embellishments, misrepresentations, or distortions that give a false impression of a person. False light claims are said to be more about the mental anguish of the person being falsely portrayed, while defamation actions are about reputational injuries. To use our hypothetical, Earl might sue based on the claim that Mary caused him grief and embarrassment due to the false light in which he was presented. He could do this even if he weren't a chef and his professional reputation didn't suffer a bit.

Either way, I'm guessing that, as an artist, these are the kinds of lawsuits you'd probably rather avoid. As you can imagine, getting sued for defamation is no fun, and, if you're found guilty, the First Amendment won't help you. Defamation, as you've probably guessed, is not protected speech. So, no matter what type of art you practice, it couldn't hurt to pay a little special attention here.

An important thing to know is that defamation operates on something of a sliding scale, depending on who's the subject of the alleged defamation. When it comes to public officials or other public figures (people who have either willingly thrust themselves into the public eye or who have been thrust there by circumstances), our judicial system recognizes that the general public has an interest in what these people do. As such, the courts are reluctant to frighten off those who would report on them by making it too easy for a factual slip-up to result in a defamation suit. So a public official or public figure can only win a defamation action if he can, first, show that the statement was indeed *false* and, second, that the statement was made with *actual malice*. In this context, "actual malice" isn't a reference to ill will. Rather, it means that the person making the statement either *knew* it was false or acted in *reckless disregard* of its falsity by not making a proper effort to determine whether or not it was true. That's the big safety net that saves the news media from being hauled into court every time they publish a piece of information about a public figure that later turns out not to be accurate.

Who constitutes a public official or public figure? Well, some are pretty easy. When it comes to *public officials*, anyone in public office or anyone running for public office can qualify as a public official. Yes, I realize that not everyone running for public office actually gets elected to public office. But, for the purposes of defamation issues, simply putting oneself into the race is the kind of voluntary act that's looked upon as sufficient to justify considering that candidate the equivalent of a public official. After all, new candidates tend to get about as much media coverage as do the incumbents.

As for nonelected government employees, they don't all count as public officials when you're talking about a defamation action. It's more often limited to those government employees who have substantial responsibility to conduct governmental business. An assistant to an assistant to an assistant deputy might not cut it. However, judges and law enforcements officers typically are viewed in defamation actions as public officials.

Public figures are a little tougher to pinpoint. But there are still some guidelines. The two basic categories of public figures are:

1. Those who occupy positions of pervasive power and influence; and

2. Otherwise private individuals who voluntarily thrust themselves into the center of a public controversy for the purpose of influencing some outcome.

As you've probably already guessed, A-List celebrities qualify. These are the performers, athletes, media personalities, and the like who have chosen to put themselves in the limelight for all the benefits that come with that notoriety. Their fame and ability to command attention just by being themselves makes them consummate public figures, whether they like it or not. Others who put themselves in the spotlight for causes that become major public issues can also turn into celebrities in their own right. You see them on the news regularly. They're quoted often. Their faces become instantly recognizable. They, too, might be classified as public figures. Less frequently, but certainly not impossibly, a person can involuntarily become a public figure through circumstances beyond that person's will or control. An example might be an airline pilot who successfully lands a disabled jumbo jet and, in so doing, becomes an instant celebrity by virtue of the action that saved the lives of everyone on board. When the jet took off, the pilot was a virtual unknown. When it landed, the pilot was a hero whose name was suddenly known around the country. At least for the duration of the public's memory about the incident, that pilot might then be considered a public figure. As with just about everything else, the final determination is probably going to be very fact-specific. But, once it's determined that someone is a public figure, that person will have to prove "actual malice" if he wants to win his claim that someone has committed actionable defamation against him.

In contrast, *private figures* have a lower hurdle to clear in proving defamation. These people, because they're not in the public eye and the events of their lives are not typically a matter of public concern, have a greater expectation of privacy. Rather than requiring proof of actual malice—a high hurdle—private figures need only prove that the person defaming them was negligent in ascertaining the truth. The lesson to be learned: While there are no guarantees when you go to court, you're on much surer legal footing if the subject at the heart of your contested statement is a public figure rather than a private one.

As we said, defamation is an injury to a person's reputation. Therefore, the amount of damages to be paid in compensation for defamation would likely be assessed based on the effect that reputational injury had on the subject. For this reason, there are some people who are considered *libel-proof* by virtue of the fact that their reputations are already so notoriously bad that the additional defamation could hardly be said to have mattered. A convicted serial killer, for example, would be in a bad position to prove his reputation had been further damaged if someone also called him a "liar." Don't count too heavily on this one, though. Truly libel-proof plaintiffs aren't all that common.

Generally speaking, government agencies cannot sue for defamation. However, *business entities* can suffer injury to their reputations and could sue for any damages their trade suffers as a result of being defamed. To go back to our hypothetical scenario, the restaurant that hired Earl might lose a lot of business as a result of people reading Mary's book and drawing the conclusion that the named restaurant doesn't do a good job of supervising its employees or checking their credentials. If Mary's assertions about Earl are inaccurate, the restaurant might be in a position to sue for the undeserved loss of its standing in the community as a quality dining establishment.

But what if Mary fictionalized Earl in her book? Would that get her off the hook as to any charges of defamation?

Well, like we said before when we were talking about other rights of real people, it depends on how recognizable Earl would be in the book. If people who know Earl would be able to recognize him from the descriptions in the book, that's not going to provide Mary with much protection should Earl take her to court. Fictionalized or not, the damage to Earl's reputation is the same if people readily know that Mary's really talking about him.

But what happens if Earl is no longer living?

In the United States, the common law has long held that you can't defame the dead. Once a person has died, his right to defend his reputation has died with him. This has been interpreted by many people as a creative green light to rewrite history in order to spice up stories they're telling about people of the past. Sometimes it means a deceased person is presented in an unflattering and undeserved light. Some have likened that to literary character assassination.

There were news stories not long after the 1997 release of the film *Titanic* about how one apparently noble officer was redrawn in the movie into a character who ran amok on the deck of the sinking ship. That depiction displeased some historians, the man's surviving family, and the officer's home town in Scotland. According to news reports, after people complained, the studio sent about $8,000 to the officer's home town as a conciliatory donation for a scholarship fund.[36] It should be noted that, despite the donation, there's nothing that says the studio ever apologized for taking the liberties it did or that it admitted any wrongdoing.

Although the law seems quite clear that there's no defamation of the dead, I urge artists (who might not have an extra eight thousand bucks lying around to assuage the feelings of ticked off descendants) to tread very cautiously in this area. It's one thing to be able to say you have the law on your side; it's another entirely to have to pay for the privilege of proving it in court. While they might not be able to file a defamation claim on behalf of a dead family member, heirs might still be able to bring a claim in their own right for infliction of emotional distress that they, themselves, have suffered as a result of the defaming references made about their deceased relative. For example, how does one live down—blatantly untrue though it might be—an assertion that your late parents were cannibals? Would anyone who believed it ever accept another dinner invitation from you?

In some cases, people who were closely involved with the deceased might also claim they've been defamed themselves by implication. For instance, if you were to write a false and libelous accusation, such as one that suggested my late father was the kingpin of a family crime syndicate, my father's not here to charge you with defaming his character. But the reference to it being a "family" crime syndicate could, by implication, extend to me as one of his family members. That could harm my reputation by

---

36   The article attributed to Reuters is available at www.titanic-titanic.com/william_murdoch.shtml.

causing people to think that I was involved in criminal activity, and it could give me grounds to sue.

The unjustly besmirched character of a deceased person might also give rise to a lawsuit if the false statement results in an economic loss to a family business or foundation. Upon hearing the defaming statements, people might no longer wish to do business or make donations to an entity associated with the memory of the departed. That's a tangible economic loss and a potential ground for a defamation suit on behalf of the business or foundation suffering the loss.

Additionally, where heirs are offended by the way a deceased family member has been portrayed in creative works, they might just fall back on the *right of publicity* doctrine as a means of litigating. Descendants of the long dead may not have this option, but those who are heirs of the recently deceased might be able to make their case stick if you're commercially appropriating their relative's name or likeness without permission. The number of years an heir can make a claim under the right of publicity doctrine depends on the law of the particular state where the deceased was residing at the time of death. So it goes without saying that it pays to know the laws of the appropriate jurisdiction before you start messing around with the dead.

There are some basic defenses to a charge of defamation. For example, if the statute of limitations runs out in the state where the defamation is said to have occurred, the would-be plaintiff is out of luck. He missed his chance.[37] And, as we've already noted, fair comment and criticism allows for even scathing critique to occur without it being fodder for a lawsuit (provided, as I said before, that it's quite obviously presented as opinion rather than fact).

Additionally, there's the defense of *consent.* If the subject consents to the publication of information about himself, knowing full well what it is you're doing, then that person takes the risk that what results might be defamatory. Note, though, that a person might consent to the initial publication of defamatory material and yet not consent to its republication later. In other words, a consent defense might let you get away with publishing the defamation once, but not necessarily a second time.

---

37   Statutes of limitation vary by state. They're typically between one and three years for defamation, and they usually start counting from whenever the publication of the defamation occurred.

There's one defamation defense that's a surefire winner, *if* you can prove it. That defense is *the truth*. One can only be defamed if what's been said is untrue. The truth bars someone from claiming that the portrayal of him has been a misrepresentation. The truth might hurt, but you're under no legal obligation to cover up someone else's shortcomings or misdeeds. Those are simply the facts.

However, take heed that the surest defense is not merely that the statement be the truth but that it be a *provable* truth. If you can't prove it's true, then it's just one person's word against another's, and that's not nearly as strong a shield. Additionally, merely attributing the statement to someone else who "says he knows," "ought to know," "must know," etc., is not going to get you off the hook automatically from a defamation charge. It's helpful evidence, but it's not incontrovertible proof. Ask any journalism editor, and he'll tell you that it's incumbent on the person writing the story to verify the facts before publishing defaming material. In a society that deems a person innocent until proven guilty, it's not sufficient simply to make accusations and then challenge the defamed individual to prove you wrong.

One last thought about this...please don't forget what we covered about *real people* in a previous chapter. Even if what you're saying is true and provable, and, therefore, not defamation, that doesn't necessarily mean that all other possibilities for legal action have automatically vanished. Right of privacy, right of publicity, and any other rights an individual might have in the use or protection of his own likeness is something that still needs to be taken into consideration by the practicing artist. It's a lot of stuff to have to keep in mind, I know. But, it's better to deal with it during the *creation* phase than during the *litigation* phase—and, usually, much cheaper, too.

How Does the Artist Protect Intellectual Property?

Perhaps it's a bizarre little quirk of human nature that causes the dichotomy of simultaneous exhibitionism and guardedness. It's the age-old situation of the child who holds out something and says "Look what I've got!" and then pulls it back the instant another child thrusts out a hand in hopes of gaining a closer inspection. Like the child with a precious bauble, the artist desires to show off his treasured art. It's the artist's way of saying, "Look at me! Look at what I've done! Isn't it wonderful!" But, despite that, the moment that art is out in the open, the artist may immediately begin fretting over the possibility that someone else will come along and steal it. We want people to admire what we've done artistically, but the very people whose admiration we crave are also people we instinctively fear as potential villains who could spoil the day through nefarious misappropriation of our life's work. This makes us tentative about sharing, lest we share with the wrong people or unintentionally give away too much, and it causes some artists to exercise a level of secrecy about what they do.

But how can the artist share his vision and exploit his work if he doesn't make it readily available to others? Therein lies the conundrum of the artist.

The schoolyard-reminiscent warning of "Look but don't touch!" is a phrase that may encapsulate the essence of this desire to show but still maintain control, and it's the basis of what we'll delve into in this chapter. There are certain protections the artist can employ and certain laws that guard against misappropriation of an artist's work. Understanding what they are and how one uses them might help us get past some of the fears and let us feel a bit more comfortable about letting others get close enough to *touch* our art, in a literal or figurative sense.

Copyright Notice and Registration

We start this discussion by going back to our old friend, copyright.

As we've already noted in an early chapter, as of January 1, 1978, there was no longer any need to file a formal registration in order to claim the copyright on an original work. Merely fixing it in some tangible medium that allows it to be shared with others creates an automatic copyright. All of the rights and privileges of copyright vest immediately without your having to fill out a single form or even notify anyone else of the work's existence. What's more, a copyright exists in a work regardless of whether or not the word "copyright" even appears on it. The bottom line is this: as I sit here on the day of this writing, typing these words into this text, my words are blessed with immediate protections conveyed by the United States Congress and backed up by the authority of the Constitution. I need do nothing more to claim those protections. It is the state of grace into which all creative works are now born in this country.

Regardless of whether the work has been officially registered with the U.S. Copyright Office, you can if you like—and it's typically a good idea—put the world on notice that you are the owner of the copyright by affixing to the work the standard notification. The notification wording contains:

- Either the symbol ©, or the word "Copyright," or the abbreviation "Copr."; and

- The year of first publication (that is, the year it was first made available for distribution to others); and

- The copyright owner's name (or an abbreviation or other designation by which the copyright owner can be recognized).

There's no statutory sequence demanded of the required information in the notice. However, most people do follow the above order. (An example of a standard copyright notice is: © 2009 Richard Amada.) You don't need any special permission to put a copyright notice on your work. Just slap it on and know that you've made known to everyone who comes in contact with it your intention to exercise copyright protections.

There's also a special notification for phonorecords of sound recordings. It's:

- The symbol ℗ ; followed by

- The year of first publication of the sound recording; followed by

- The name of the owner of the sound recording's copyright.

You need to position the copyright notice somewhere on the copies being distributed in such a way that it gives reasonable notice of your claim to anyone who comes in contact with those copies. By statute, if the notice is properly displayed, a court will give no weight to a defendant's assertion that he was an innocent who just didn't know he was infringing the copyright on that work. The benefit of that to you, as the copyright holder, is that you might be able to collect additional damages from someone who's not able to prove he was an "innocent infringer."[38]

The potential penalties a court could impose for copyright infringement include:

- An injunction preventing further distribution of the infringing copies;
- An order impounding or destroying all the infringing copies;
- An award of costs and attorney's fees to the copyright owner; and
- Either:
    a) an award of actual damages suffered by the copyright owner as a result of the infringement, as well as any profits of the infringer attributable to the infringing activity, or
    b) Instead of actual damages and profits, the copyright owner may elect to receive an award of statutory damages (currently ranging anywhere from $750 to $30,000). If the copyright owner can prove that the defendant infringed the copyright willfully, the court has the option of increasing the statutory damages (currently up to $150,000). However, if the infringer can prove he wasn't aware, and had no reason to believe his acts constituted copyright infringement, the court could reduce the statutory damages award (currently to as low as $200).

Additionally, there are possible criminal charges that can be made against a willful infringer who:

- purposefully commits copyright infringement for commercial advantage or private financial gain, or;

---

38   The statute governing Notice of Copyright is 17 U.S.C. § 401. Specific examples of methods and locations for affixing copyright notice are contained in the Code of Federal Regulations, 37 C.F.R. § 201.20. It's available on the Copyright Office website at www.copyright.gov/title37, under "General Provisions."

- who, within a 180-day period, willfully reproduces or distributes infringing copies or phonorecords whose total retail value is more than $1,000, or;
- who willfully makes someone else's copyrighted work available to the general public on a computer network when, in fact, that infringer knew or should have known that the copyrighted work was intended for commercial distribution.[39]

That last one, a fairly recent addition to the law, is a nod to the growing copyright protection difficulties related to Internet file swapping. Most, if not all of us, have become keenly aware of this situation. For example, if Steve uploads onto the web a pirated copy of Joby's new music release for anyone to download and listen to for *free*, how many people are going to bother going to a commercial distributor's site where they'll have to pay to hear it? Joby's song could be a big hit, and she might still end up losing money because her ability to market the release commercially was taken away from her by Steve, who went into competition with her by distributing the music for a price she couldn't beat: *zippo*. If Joby was hoping to make a lot of money on the release of her song, you can readily understand why she'd have a beef with Steve and why she'd be inclined to take legal action against him.

But what if Steve doesn't actually upload the music to his website but, instead, simply creates a site designed to allow others to illegally upload and download copyright-protected material? Can Steve be sued for that? The answer is *yes*, under the legal theory of *contributory infringement*. It's a form of vicarious liability in which a person who knowingly allows the infringement to take place can be held liable for the resulting damages.[40] Contributory infringement is by no means limited to acts on the Internet. It can happen anywhere when someone has knowledge that infringing activity is going on and, with that knowledge, induces, causes, or materially contributes to it—even if that person is not directly committing copyright infringement himself. Courts have found contributory infringement in various cases, including one where the manager of performing artists know-

---

39   More information about copyright infringement's civil and criminal remedies is contained in the Copyright Act, 17 U.S.C. §§ 501 – 513.

40   See *A&M Records v. Napster*, discussed on pp. 125–6.

ingly allowed those artists to perform unlicensed music in public[41] and, also, a case where a publisher distributed a doll-making instruction booklet that the publisher knew would be used to create infringing copies of copyright protected dolls.[42] (We'll get into contributory infringement a bit more when we discuss Internet piracy later in this chapter.)

Before you can bring an infringement action against someone, you first need to have officially registered the work with the U.S. Copyright Office. You don't need to have registered it prior to the infringing action. This is important, so I'll repeat it. *You don't need to have registered the work prior to the infringing action in order to sue someone for copyright infringement of that work.* If someone infringes your copyright privileges on your *un*registered work, you can still take legal action against that infringer. But, before you file the case, you first need to register the work officially with the Copyright Office.[43]

Going back to our example of Joby and Steve, let's say Joby hasn't yet registered the song or the recording of the song with the Copyright Office. Now along comes Steve who puts a pirated copy of the recording on his website. As we know from our earlier discussion, failing to register a copyright doesn't deprive Joby of any of her rights as the copyright holder. Steve's action is copyright infringement, pure and simple, and Joby's got grounds to go to court. In this case, though, her first stop will be to file the necessary documents with the Copyright Office to register her song. (She could register both the music and the recording of it as two separate registrations.) Once that's done, she's then free to bring a legal action against Steve for his infringement of her music, even though that infringement occurred prior to Joby's registration.

However, there is a significant downside to waiting to register one's work until after an infringement has occurred. Under Section 412 of the Copyright Act, no award of statutory damages or attorney's fees can be collected by the copyright owner for any infringement that occurs prior to the

---

41   *Gershwin Publishing Corp. v. Columbia Artists Management*, heard by the U.S. Second Circuit Court of Appeals in 1971.

42   *Original Appalachian Artworks v. Cradle Creations*, heard by a U.S. District Court in the Northern District of Georgia in 1983.

43   This is governed by 17 U.S.C. § 411.

work being officially registered with the Copyright Office.[44] In the absence of statutory damages, a plaintiff is left to prove *actual damages* suffered, or actual ill-gotten profits reaped by the defendant, in order to derive a dollar figure that a court could award as compensation. Attempting to determine actual damages and actual profits can be a rather speculative business, and it's often hard to prove what you *would have earned* had your work not been stolen. That being the case, the ability to collect statutory damages and attorney's fees is a pretty strong incentive for registering your work before you shop it around or put it in general circulation.

Registering a work with the Copyright Office is simple. Basically, you fill in a short form, pay the fee, and submit a sample of the work. Published works require two samples, and, for those works in which copies aren't easily deposited (e.g., sculptures, paintings), a photograph of it will typically do. You can do the whole thing online now at *www.copyright.gov/register*, and they charge you less if you do it online than if you do it with the old paper forms. The only thing the examiners at the Copyright Office will do with your application is check to see if the material deposited with them meets the criteria for copyrightable subject matter, and they'll determine if all the formal requirements for the submission have been met. Beyond that, the Copyright Office operates under a "rule of doubt" doctrine in which a work will be registered so long as there's at least a reasonable doubt in their minds as to whether or not the work is copyrightable. Very little that's submitted for registration is rejected by the Copyright Office. If for some reason something you've submitted does get rejected, you can appeal the decision to the Copyright Office Board of Appeals.

Evidence of Original Authorship

One of the things artists routinely fret about is the possibility that someone will infringe their copyright, and the artist won't be able to prove that his own art is the original and the infringer's is an illegal copy. While there's no requirement that a work be unique to attain a copyright, should the issue arise regarding *who copied whom*, it may become necessary for the artist to prove that his work was already in existence and available for copying at the time of the infringement. The primary elements to proving copyright

---

44   In the case of a *published* work, the registration must take place within three months of its first publication to qualify for statutory damages and attorney's fees on an infringement that occurs after publication.

infringement are: (1) that the infringer had access to the work, and (2) that the infringer then copied it. Remember the case where George Harrison's song, *My Sweet Lord*, was found to be an infringement of the melody of *He's So Fine*?[45] The key to that case was that Mr. Harrison couldn't deny that he had access to the earlier song, which he had heard when it was being played on the radio some years before. Although no one really suspected that he had deliberately set out to copy someone else's music, the fact that Mr. Harrison had heard that song, and later produced a strikingly similar melody, was all that was needed to declare *My Sweet Lord* an infringing copy.

In the case of less notable or unpublished works, the key question is: How does one prove the infringer had the requisite access to the work if there's no official record of the work having been around during the relevant time period?

As we've already noted, the Copyright Office makes no effort to verify that what's submitted for registration is, in fact, an original work. Therefore, official copyright registration is *not* proof of original authorship. However, it can at least be rebuttable evidence to that effect. Section 410(c) of the Copyright Act states:

> *In any judicial proceedings the certificate of a registration made before or within five years after first publication of the work shall constitute prima facie evidence of the validity of the copyright and of the facts stated in the certificate. The evidentiary weight to be accorded the certificate of a registration made thereafter shall be within the discretion of the court.*

If you're not familiar with the term *"prima facie* evidence"—and virtually no one other than lawyers has any reason to be—it simply means that it's evidence which is sufficient and good *on its face*. That means, if you register your art before or within five years of making it available for distribution, someone else has the burden of proving in court that you weren't the first to create that work. If you wait more than five years to register it, a court determining originality of authorship can still take that registration into account, but it doesn't have to count it as *prima facie* evidence, which means the evidence isn't as strong. This is another factor that weighs in favor of register-

---

45   See pp. 50-51.

ing your work with the Copyright Office whenever you feel the work has the potential for marketability.

Because *prima facie* evidence is *rebuttable*—that is, it can be overcome by other evidence that disproves it—official copyright registration is no guarantee that your work will be declared the first of its kind in an infringement dispute. For this reason, artists have long sought other means of making an indisputable record of their work's date of creation. The results of this search have been a mixed bag.

Among the methods devised by artists is something commonly referred to as the "poor man's copyright." The way it works is this: The artist puts a copy of his work in a sealed envelope and then mails it to himself. When the post office delivers the envelope, the artist leaves it sealed and puts it away for safekeeping. Should an issue later arise over when that work was created, the artist can then produce the sealed envelope to the court as evidence of the existence of the envelope's contents as of the date of the postmark. Proponents of this method note that it's cheaper and quicker than official copyright registration, and, since the Copyright Office doesn't verify originality anyway, this is one means of getting the federal government to indirectly corroborate a work's existence on a specific date.

While the poor man's copyright might fall into a "better than nothing" category, it's hardly conclusive proof. The problem is that it's too easy to fake such things, and the postmaster isn't going to be able to testify on your behalf that the envelope and its contents are thoroughly legitimate and haven't been tampered with. What's more, I'm aware of no case in which the poor man's copyright has been used successfully to prove that one work infringed another—and I've looked. With that in mind, I can't truly recommend this approach to copyright protection.

A better alternative might be the so-called *non-repudiation services*. These are entities that allow artists to "file" a copy of their art with the service, which then records the date of receipt and promises to verify the art's having existed on that date should the issue ever come up. This has been a longtime practice of the Writer's Guild of America, which offers the service, for a fee, to writers who want to make a formal record of their work before they begin shopping it around. It's a fairly common practice for screenwriters to utilize the Writer's Guild's non-repudiation service because, regardless of whether or not it's deserved, Hollywood has a notorious reputation when it comes to stealing ideas.

Similar services for other artists have sprung up. You can find such non-repudiation services on the Internet, and some advertise themselves as free. Among the services they offer is a digital date/time stamp on works that are in digital format. While this is certainly a step up from the poor man's copyright—it's an impartial third party who can make the assertion on the artist's behalf—these digital stamps might not always be a foolproof option. Digital data can be manipulated by those who know the technology well enough. That means, for a digital non-repudiation service's testimony to carry really significant weight in a court of law, it will need to demonstrate that its database is immune to tampering. At the moment, those are untested waters in our legal system, and so the verdict may not be fully in on the usefulness of such digital stamps.

Unfair Competition Protections

If I say to you, "golden arches," what comes to mind?

If it takes you longer than three seconds to respond "McDonald's," then may I be among the first to welcome you back from the desert island on which you've been marooned for the past several decades.

For the rest of us, the golden arches inspire one automatic, practically Pavlovian response. Love 'em or hate 'em, you've got to admit there's no mistaking them. The McDonald's food franchise is globally recognized by that simple, yellow-gold, double-humped emblem that appears on the packaging of pretty much everything it produces. When you come across that trademark logo, it's only natural that you'd assume you've come in contact with a product of the McDonald's Corporation. If someone who's not affiliated with McDonald's were to slap a confusingly similar logo onto his own products, it's highly likely that people would mistake the non-affiliated products for those of the well-known chain because, in the general public's mind, the golden arches have taken on a secondary meaning associated specifically with McDonald's. This is the sort of confusion that trademark law is designed to prevent, and you can bet McDonald's lawyers would be all over the imitator faster than the Hamburgler on a Big Mac.

Similarly, if someone were to start using a slogan that's confusingly similar to an already established slogan of a competitor, that, too, could give rise to legal action by the competitor wishing to protect itself from having its customers deceptively lured away by an imposter. There's only one circus that gets to call itself "The Greatest Show on Earth."

However, legal protections aren't limited to just logos and words. They also apply to something called *trade dress*. That's defined as a combination of elements that comprise the total image of the product—things like size, shape, texture, graphic elements, or colors (so long as these things are stylistic choices and not functionally necessary). For example, the UPS company has gone to great lengths to make the color brown synonymous with its delivery service. It's the color of its corporate logo, the color of its uniforms, and the color that it paints its trucks. The company has gone so far as to refer to itself in its advertising as "Brown." (E.g., "What can Brown do for you?") This type of ad campaign is designed specifically to give the color brown a secondary meaning that's associated in the package delivery industry only with UPS. Furthermore, while it might seem odd to some that a company could claim dibs officially on something as common as a simple color, UPS has registered its particular chocolate brown color on the U.S. trademark registry. One might ask, does that mean no one else in the country can ever utilize a similar color brown in a commercial pursuit? (After all, there are only so many colors in the visual spectrum.) No, it doesn't mean that. But that commercial pursuit better not be the package delivery business, or that business will likely be hearing from UPS's lawyers.

So what does all this have to do with you as an artist?...*Everything*, if you happen to be an artist who intends to sell your art in a competitive market.

Let's say Patti is a distinguished dancer who runs *Patti's Dance Studio* where she gives ballet and tap lessons to children. Word gets around about how good Patti's classes are, and soon parents all over town are calling to enroll their children. Then sometime later a new dance studio opens up in town—this one calling itself *Patty's Dance Studio*. The similarity between *Patti* (with an "i" on the end) and *Patty* (with a "y" on the end) is relatively negligible in the minds of the parents who simply heard about a great dance school run by someone named Patti. Whether those parents will think to inquire as to whether the name they want has an "i" or a "y" on the end of it is debatable, and they might not think twice about it when they spot an ad for one studio and just dial the number they see there. The disservice here is twofold. One, the parents could be sending their children to a school that's different from the one they wanted (the one with the great reputation), and, two, the original Patti may be losing out on business not because she did anything wrong but, rather, just because someone else is now capitalizing on the goodwill Patti built for her own business.

Whether you're running a dance class, an art studio, a theater company, a video production company, or any other arts-related business, the marketability of what you do could depend a great deal on the reputation you create for yourself. People seeking such services may be drawn to you specifically because of that reputation. If some copycat comes along and markets his art in a deceptively similar manner—using a similar name, logo, slogan, or trade dress—in order to steal your potential customers by capitalizing on the goodwill you've created for yourself, it hardly seems fair.

Therefore, in addition to copyright and trademark, the artist can also turn to *unfair competition* laws for further protection. If someone employs such unfair practices to your economic detriment, you might be able to take legal action under federal and/or state laws. The remedies available for such actions could include both monetary damages and the possibility of a court-issued injunction ordering the other party to cease the unfair trade practices.

That said, please don't confuse unfair competition laws with any restrictions on the legal free enterprise system. The fundamental right to freely compete on the open market is the very basis of our economy, and there is absolutely nothing in the law that says someone can't set up a business that directly competes with you and that attempts to win over the clientele that otherwise might have patronized your business. Legal commercial practices can include those things that would naturally have a negative impact on competitors—including making unflattering comparisons.

> *"You'd have to eat fifty bowls of that other cereal to get the fiber contained in just one bowl of End Result!"*

That's just the way of the free market, and the ones who either offer the best wares or do the best job of marketing them are the ones who will survive. Unfair competition laws come into play only where there is some deception being practiced on the general public such that there's a reasonable chance people will be confused as to the source of the product or service they're seeking.

Questions regarding public confusion sometimes arise in connection with the titles of creative works. Since titles aren't copyrightable, and you can't trademark a title unless it's being used in connection with the marketing of some product or service, it's possible for two works to have similar or even identical titles without violating copyright or trademark laws. Despite that, you've probably noticed that you don't see two different books or two different movies with the same title coming out at the same time. So you're probably thinking to yourself that there must be something in the law that prevents that. And you'd be correct. The same kinds of unfair competition protections that exist for a business could also be employed to guard against public confusion when it comes to titles.

In the 1934 case, *Warner Brothers Pictures v. Majestic Pictures*, Warner Brothers sued a rival studio over the use of a similar film title. Warner Brothers had produced two film versions of the play, *The Gold Diggers*, the rights of which it had purchased from the play's author. The success of those two movies led the studio to begin production of a new film version under the title *Gold Diggers of 1933*. Much to Warner Brothers' displeasure, Majestic Pictures released a similar film that same year with the title *Gold Diggers of Paris*. The injunction Warner Brothers sought wasn't based on copyright infringement but, rather, on an unfair competition charge stemming from the defendant's use of the words "Gold Diggers" in the competing film's title. Because of the success of the previous Warner Brothers' versions, the court ruled that the use of the descriptive words, "Gold Diggers," had acquired secondary meaning in the minds of the public as a title associated with Warner Brothers' productions. That, in the court's opinion, presented a significant likelihood of public confusion regarding the source of the competing Majestic movie, and the court issued an injunction preventing Majestic from using the title.

Unfair competition, as regards titles, might be as much a matter of timing as anything else. Over the years, there have been a number of movies titled *The Great Train Robbery*, or something very similar to that. If two of them were released at the same time, how would anyone be able to look at the marquee and know which one was playing at that particular cinema?[46] If a studio has a lot of money riding on its new film, and someone else releases another film with the same title to compete with it, the likelihood of public confusion could trigger charges of unfair competition. However, if there's

---

46   In fact, after the Edison Studios released *The Great Train Robbery* in 1903, another film with the exact same title and a virtually identical story was released by another filmmaker just one year later. Apparently, Thomas Edison had bigger fish to fry and just let this pass without further action. Personally, I wouldn't count on that type of inactivity from Hollywood should a similar situation arise today.

a significant amount of time between one release and the other, the chance of confusion is greatly diminished. Making a successful claim under unfair competition laws, when the two works aren't really competing with each other, is a much tougher hill to climb. Yet, if a work retains its popularity over the years, that could be a significant factor that could be taken into account when determining whether a newer work with the same title is infringing or diluting the earlier work's marketability.

There's a rather famous story in which Warner Brothers' legal department got antsy when it heard that the Marx Brothers were making a film titled *A Night in Casablanca,* which was being shot a few years after the release of Warner Brothers' classic movie *Casablanca.* Depending on the source you read, Warner Brothers either got exasperated with the silly responses it received from Groucho, or it finally decided that the two films were different enough that the similarity of the titles didn't merit litigation. But the lesson to be taken away from all this is, if someone views a similar title as a potential economic threat to a commercially marketable property, it's not beyond all reason to envision that unfair competition charges could be forthcoming. If you're planning on writing a book with a title like *Harry Potter and the Sorcerer's Knishes,* tread carefully…and have a lawyer nearby. You'll probably need one.

In most cases, characters can't be copyrighted. However, like titles, where a character acquires secondary meaning, it can enjoy protection from another's unauthorized copying of that character. One such case involved the comic actor Charlie Chaplin and the "little tramp" character that he developed as his screen persona. The phenomenal popularity of Mr. Chaplin's onscreen performances prompted a competitor to duplicate the look and antics of the little tramp character in his own movies. Mr. Chaplin sued, and a California court ordered that the imitator cease marketing the film or anything else that would likely deceive the movie-going public into thinking that the copycat was Mr. Chaplin.[47] Again it was the likelihood of public confusion that carried the day in court. A few years earlier, in *Fisher v. Star Co.,* New York's highest court debated secondary meaning in characters and whether protections were appropriate for the cartoon characters in Bud Fisher's comic strip, *Mutt and Jeff.* After Mr. Fisher made an exclusive contract with a syndicator for the distribution of the comic strip, a New York

---

47   The case was *Chaplin v. Amador,* ruled on by the California Court of Appeals in 1928.

publisher decided to bypass Mr. Fisher and continue the strip as drawn by its own employees. The court noted that Mr. Fisher didn't claim protection based on copyright or trademark law but, rather, only on state laws regarding unfair competition. In ruling in Mr. Fisher's favor, the court wrote:

> *The figures and names have been so connected with the respondent as their originator or author that the use by another of new cartoons exploiting the characters "Mutt and Jeff" would be unfair to the public and to the plaintiff. No person should be permitted to pass off as his own the thoughts and works of another.*

The unfairness of *passing off* one thing for another is the very essence of a federal law known as Section 43(a) of the Lanham Act.[48] Originally envisioned as a statute to combat false advertising, Section 43(a) has evolved into a powerful tool to prevent one party from passing off its own work as that of another. For example, if you were to attempt to sell a photograph you had taken yourself, but which you claimed was one taken by renowned photographer Annie Leibovitz, you'd be guilty of what's commonly referred to as "passing off," and, when it occurs in interstate commerce[49], it's a violation of the Lanham Act. Much like passing off a cheap knock-off watch as a Rolex, passing off your own art as that of someone else who's more famous is clearly cheating the customer by deceiving him into buying something through false claims. The customer isn't really getting what he was led to believe he was buying. Additionally, passing off is harmful to the artist whose name is being fraudulently invoked as the creator of the false art, because it has the potential of diluting the stature of the plagiarized artist when lesser works are distributed to the public—works the quality of which the copied artist can't control. Think of what it might do to Ms. Leibovitz's professional reputation if people were to gauge the quality of her art based on photos they thought were her creations but that, in reality, were the work of an untalented amateur. You can probably well understand why she'd want to put a stop to that activity as quickly as possible.

The same section of the Lanham Act also forbids what is called *reverse passing off*. This is defined as passing off someone else's work as if it were

---

48   Codified in the United States Code as 15 U.S.C. § 1125(a).

49   And just about all buying and selling that isn't restricted to one state is interstate commerce.

your own. In this case, imagine if I were to put my name on Ms. Leibovitz's photos and sell them as my own artistic creations. Such a deceit would rob the true artist of the credit she deserves, and the Lanham Act makes that deception illegal. This applies to any of the arts and entertainment industries where attribution is standard. A writer, for example, might bring a case against a publisher under the Lanham Act if someone else's name appeared as the author on that writer's book, or an actor might invoke the Lanham Act if the producers of a movie substituted a different actor's name in the film's credits.

The use of voices, too, can be deemed an illegal misappropriation under the Lanham Act. When a well-known celebrity's voice is imitated in a sound recording, such that the general public might not know it's just an imitation, that runs the risk of creating a situation in which the recording could constitute a false endorsement—that is, it might suggest to the listeners that the actual celebrity is putting his name and reputation behind whatever is being spoken of in his mimicked voice. Unless you've got that celebrity's permission, using his notoriety to sell your product is an unauthorized infringement on the celeb's right of publicity, and it runs afoul of the Lanham Act's prohibition on false representations in the advertising of goods and services. This is why broadcast advertisements that make use of impersonations of famous people always throw in a disclaimer at the end that tells the audience it wasn't really that famous person you saw or heard in the ad (just in case you weren't absolutely certain that it wasn't actually the President of the United States hawking those foot-long sandwiches in the commercial).

Protecting the Pitch

Time now to hark back to our artists' conundrum. Remember our *look but don't touch* dichotomy? We so much want to put our art before the world, but the avenues to that goal are fraught with potholes in the form of real or imagined intellectual property thieves who make us wary and tentative. We know that we can't copyright an *idea*—no matter how brilliant or original it is—and, once that genie's out of the bottle, there's no putting it back. An idea that has been allowed to bloom in public is an idea that's available for the plucking by anyone who comes across it. This puts in a most precarious position the artist who wants to pitch an idea to a potential buyer. You've got to make the pitch to be in the game. But, once you've set your wares out on the shelves, have you given away the store?

All the cheesy metaphors aside, there's at least a reasonable chance that the subject matter I'm alluding to is one that causes you a bit of queasiness because you recognize it as a very real and sometimes distressing situation. It's particularly troublesome to aspiring artists who desperately want to break into the business but fear that the very ideas that could grant them entry would, once they're revealed, be stolen by others or simply given away to established artists to exploit instead. If there's a chance for serious money to be made, it's probably not an unreasonable fear. Although the reality of actual theft may be far more likely in some industries than in others, before marching off to that big pitch meeting, every artist ought to arm himself with a little knowledge about how one might go about protecting the pitch.

If it hasn't been made absolutely crystal clear by now, let's make sure at least one thing is understood. Section 102(b) of the Copyright Act specifically bars *ideas* from copyright protection. Only the original *expression* of ideas can be copyrighted. That doesn't mean you, as an author, can simply write on a piece of paper:

> *Boy meets girl,*
> *Boy loses girl,*
> *Boy and girl get together in the end,*

and then claim copyright ownership of all future stories based on that idea. There are no laws granting a legal monopoly on ideas that are common and general to the entire world. Even if you were to show another author the paper on which you've written your expression of your "boy meets girl" idea, and then that author wrote a novel following that exact same scenario, there's no way you'd be able to make a winning claim that the author stole your idea. The commonality of that skeletal premise, and the fact that anyone else could just as easily come up with precisely the same thing, puts it outside the realm of a protectable expression. It's merely an unprotected idea. (If "boy meets girl" isn't the oldest story premise in history, it may be second only to "boy meets saber-toothed tiger.")

Even far more detailed and specific ideas can fall prey to *legal* appropriation should those ideas get out. Case in point: *Murray v. National Broadcasting Company* involved an employee in NBC's sports division, Hwesu Murray, who in 1980 went to a programming official with some ideas he had for possible television shows. Among those ideas was a show that would star comedian Bill Cosby in a situation comedy about a middle-class,

African American family in an urban setting. The network official asked Mr. Murray to flesh out the ideas in writing, which he did. Although the network subsequently told Mr. Murray it decided not to pursue the proposal, four years later *The Cosby Show* premiered on NBC, which prompted Mr. Murray to file a lawsuit alleging that the network stole his idea. When the case went before the Second Circuit Court of Appeals, the court noted that there were indeed similarities between the plaintiff's original proposal and what NBC eventually produced as *The Cosby Show*. However, two of the court's three judges ruled that there wasn't enough novelty in the plaintiff's proposal to qualify it as a protectable piece of property under New York law. "While NBC's decision to broadcast *The Cosby Show* unquestionably was innovative in the sense that an intact, nonstereotypical black family had never been portrayed on television before," wrote Judge Frank X. Altimari in the majority opinion, "the mere fact that such a decision had not been made before does not necessarily mean that the idea for the program is itself novel." He added, "...there can be no cause of action for unauthorized use of Murray's proposal since it was not unlawful for defendants to use a non-novel idea."

If nothing else, we should take away from this story the lesson that it's no easy task to prove that you alone possess an idea that constitutes a protectable piece of property. That being the case, it's better to take whatever precautions you can *in advance of spilling the beans on a new idea.* Admittedly, the precautions available to an aspiring artist could be rather limited as compared to those available to established artists with some influence. But let's take a look at what's out there.

First, there are contractual precautions some artists use that are called *non-disclosure agreements.* These are written agreements, which basically state that the artist has some information he wishes to submit to a potential buyer, but only if the buyer will promise not to disclose the information to anyone else. Part of the agreement might contain language such as:

> *The Artist will disclose confidential information about the Artist's submission to the Potential Buyer solely for the purpose of allowing that Potential Buyer to evaluate the submission to determine, in his sole discretion, whether the submission may be further developed into a project. If the Potential Buyer determines that the submission is suitable for further development, the Artist and Potential Buyer will attempt to agree on*

a development schedule and compensation to the Artist for the submission.

The Potential Buyer agrees that, in accepting the Artist's disclosure of confidential information, the Potential Buyer will exercise the same degree of care to maintain that the confidential information is kept secret and confidential as is employed by the Potential Buyer to preserve and safeguard his own materials and confidential information. The Potential Buyer will not use the confidential information for any purpose whatsoever, other than for the sole purpose of evaluating the submission to determine whether it may be further developed into a project, unless and until a further executed agreement is first made between the Artist and the Potential Buyer setting forth the terms and conditions under which the rights to the Artist's submission and confidential information are licensed to or acquired by the Potential Buyer.

Obviously, if a buyer is part of a corporation where more than one person would be involved in the buying decision, you're going to have to allow that buyer to tell others about what you're trying to sell. The purpose of a non-disclosure agreement, really, is just to prevent that buyer from blabbing to others who aren't involved in the decision and have no need to know about your carefully guarded idea.

Foolproof? Hardly. But it's a step in the right direction *if* you can get a potential buyer to agree to it. And that's a big *if.* If you're Steven Spielberg pitching a motion picture idea to Universal Studios, you've probably got the clout to get a studio exec's signature on a non-disclosure agreement. If you're Ernie the screenwriter, without a sold movie script to your name, chances are the studio would rather just forgo the opportunity of hearing your idea than to commit to a contract that gives you legal options. The reason for this is that movie studios, as well as other corporate buyers of intellectual property, don't want to put themselves in the position of promising not to use any idea of yours before they know what that idea is. There are so many similar ideas out there that it's entirely possible the studio could already have one in the works that's very much like Ernie's, and the last thing that studio wants to have happen is to be forced to halt an existing project because it signed a contract with Ernie promising not to do any movies involving anything resembling the idea he pitched. This is the unfortunate reality that puts so many artists in a virtually powerless position when it comes to negotiating non-disclosure agreements.

A second, and often more attainable protection for artists, is something generally referred to as *industry custom*. Regardless of whether or not you, yourself, have a track record as a professional artist, if you're dealing with a potential buyer who's in a business that routinely *purchases* such ideas, there's a reasonable expectation that the buyer will compensate the artist for any of the artist's ideas the buyer decides to use.

Let's go back to our example of the movie pitch. Screenwriter Ernie isn't about to take his new action movie treatment to a studio exec just for the satisfaction of having the exec proclaim the treatment good enough to steal. Ernie expects that, if the studio makes the movie, Ernie will get paid and receive proper billing in the film credits. What's more, the studio exec knows that, too. One can only imagine the laughter that would break out in a courtroom if that exec were to testify that he honestly believes that people bring him movie ideas all the time without their ever expecting anything in return other than to allow that exec to get richer off of their ideas. *Please!* It's a business. And "business" means people get compensated for their work. If a buyer routinely pays for the ideas he appropriates from others, that's the industry custom. Courts have interpreted the understandings and expectations of both sides of such custom as a sort of unwritten contract that's implied by the facts. If someone in the industry invites you, or accepts your invitation to hear you pitch an idea, and that industry professional then appropriates the idea without your permission, proper attribution, or compensation, you might be able to make a case against him for breach of an implied contract. As admissible evidence, implied contracts aren't typically as strong as express written contracts, but they are legally enforceable when proven to exist.

There are no guaranteed safeguards when it comes to a non-copyright-able commodity like an idea. So it may be that the best one can do when peddling ideas is simply to take as many precautions as you're able.

First and foremost, create a paper trail. As we noted earlier in this chapter, registering your work with either the Copyright Office, or one of the other registries, provides evidence of the existence of the work as of the registration date. That could be important if a question arises over whose work was created first. However, remember, that alone doesn't prove some-one else had access to your work or copied from it. Keep a record of the names, positions, and contact information of anyone to whom you're providing confidential information, and note the dates (and times, if appropriate) that information was provided. If the information is going by mail, send it by some method that allows for it to be tracked or that requires a signature on the receiving end so that you know when and by whom it was received. Charges of misappropriation require proof that the defendant had actual access to what is alleged to have been stolen. You need to be able to document who came in contact with your work.[50]

Written submissions typically make stronger evidence than do verbal ones. However, if the pitch takes place in person or by phone, follow it up with a confirmation letter that memorializes the key elements of what was discussed. This could be important later should a dispute arise over what was said or agreed to during the discussion. If the potential buyer disagrees with your version of what transpired between you, let him make his objections known while you're giving him the chance. If he waits until an actual dispute arises to voice objections to your understanding (as expressed in the letter), those objections might be viewed as weakened by his failure to voice them sooner.

Finally, while it may seem crass to talk about money when someone's showing interest in your art, it's even more crass to *fight about money* later. Whenever you're making a pitch to a potential buyer, it's in your best interest to let that person know—delicately, though you might phrase it—that your proposal is an offer to attempt to make a business deal. If the buyer you're dealing with is a businessperson, that buyer ought to understand and take no offense. It's nothing personal. It's just business.

Dealing with Internet Piracy

It's difficult for me to think of any place where there are more misconceptions, misunderstandings, misdirection, and misappropriations than the

---

50   Under something called the "Corporate Receipt Doctrine," possession of a work by one employee of a corporation implies possession of that work by another employee of the same corporation. So a corporation can't escape misappropriation charges simply by handing off confidential information from one employee who had direct contact with the artist to another employee who did not have that direct contact. However, to prevail in court, it's not enough just to allege that one employee must have gotten your work from another simply because they work for the same company. Lots of companies have various divisions and branches that never have any reason to communicate with each other. To make a convincing argument, you need to show that the employee who misappropriated your work had a reasonable possibility of viewing or hearing it.

Internet. The very fact that we routinely capitalize the word "Internet"—which, as best as I can make out, is not a proper noun—suggests to me that there's some genuine confusion among us as to exactly what the properties of the cyber world are and how the rules apply to it. The Internet has been compared to the Wild West or the lawless open seas, and, because there's no central government office responsible for it, I can readily understand how that image is able to be perpetuated. However, the Internet isn't as wild and lawless as some might think. The laws that govern us don't magically evaporate into the Ethernet (another curiously capitalized word). They remain in full force, just as they would in any other medium, including those that apply to acts in foreign lands that are enforceable through treaties. That includes the laws of copyright.

I know this will come as a major shock to many of you, but just try to get your head around this concept: A digital online file of text, images, or sound can be legally downloaded to another computer or similar digital device *only with the permission of the copyright owner.*

Yes, I know this sounds bizarre to those of you who are accustomed to just right-clicking on a website and saving files to your own computer. It's how you got all those funny digital pictures you share with your friends. It's so darned easy, and the computer manufacturers build the capability right into the computer, so how could it possibly be illegal? Well, technically speaking, it is.

To better understand, let's look at it another way. Let's say you've shot some photos of you and your family on a vacation adventure in Japan. Since you took the photos, the copyright on those images belongs to you. No argument so far, right?

Now let's say one of those photos is a picture of your daughter, Kathryn, standing next to a sumo wrestler. When you get home, you can't wait to upload that photo onto your blog. And there it is—a few clicks, and Kathryn and the sumo wrestler are cruising down the information superhighway for all the world to see.

What have you done? Have you abandoned your copyright on the image? *Absolutely not.* Have you given away your right to market that image if you can find someone who wants to buy it? *Not a bit.* Have you given up your family's rights of privacy and publicity? Well, any privacy you might have desired for keeping secret that trip to Japan is out the window once you put the photo on public display (as it would be with any photo displayed publicly anywhere), but the rest of your family's rights remain intact. You don't forfeit your legal rights by publishing something online anymore than you'd forfeit those rights through any other type of publication. They're still your rights. And what that means is that you, as the owner of the copyright on that photo, are the only person in the world who is legally permitted to make, or authorize the making of copies of it. The Copyright Act doesn't limit its definition of "copies" to just those made in the forms of solid media like paper. *Digital copies* count, too. When you download a file from a remote site, the end result is that the bits of information that make up that file have been transmitted as a digital copy to a new database, and now that file exists in a brand new place where it had not existed before (namely, your computer or other digital device). With that newly created file on your computer, you now have the ability to do such things as distribute it through online sharing, burn it onto CD/DVD, or print it to paper, just as if you had the original source file. Therefore, downloading a digital file from one database and saving it onto another is legally defined as *making a copy* of the original. And, as we know, only the copyright owner possesses the legal right to do that. Therefore, in the absence of permission from the copyright owner, it's a violation of copyright law to download someone else's intellectual property from one database to another. It amounts to Internet piracy.

Now, to put your mind at rest, I'm not patrolling cyberspace, cracking down on people who download someone else's online vacation photos. Nor am I aware of anyone else who's doing anything even remotely like that sort of policing. Yes, technically, it's a violation. But, realistically, it goes on so many times every minute of every day, without it causing any appreciable harm, that most people just don't care. What's more, if there's no commercial value in the property, you're unlikely to find someone who will go to great lengths to crack down on that sort of rather trivial theft. (You probably weren't planning to sell that photo of Kathryn and the Sumo wrestler anyway. What's more, unless you're a professional photographer, you probably didn't think to get that Sumo wrestler's signature on a release form. Did you?...I thought not.)

However, if you're an artist, you might care very much that people are just downloading unauthorized copies of your art for free rather than purchasing the art wherever it's meant to be sold. That's money out of your pocket, and it's the double-edged sword that is the digital age. It offers unparalleled opportunities for getting your art *out there* by way of instantaneous global publishing, but it also unleashes an almost unstoppable deluge of copyright infringement—most of that infringement taking place without the infringers even realizing they're doing anything wrong. It just doesn't occur to most people that there could be anything illegal about uploading or downloading something they can access freely on the web. And that's giving the entertainment industry fits. In particular, the music industry is practically beside itself over the loss of potential revenues resulting from digital music sharing—known as *peer-to-peer file sharing*—that turns one legally sold copy into who-knows-how-many unauthorized freebie copies with the click of a button.

Chasing down every individual who downloads an unauthorized song or movie is functionally impractical because of the sheer number of people doing it, and because they're literally spread all over the planet. So, more often than not, the entertainment industry focuses its attempts to crack down on online infringement by targeting the people who make the infringement possible—the contributory infringers, about whom we talked earlier in this chapter.

As I said before, for someone to be found guilty of contributory copyright infringement, he must knowingly induce, cause, or materially contribute to the infringing behavior. The key word here is *knowingly*. An Internet Service Provider (ISP) that doesn't know that its web space is being used by others to carry on illegal copying cannot be held liable for contributory infringement. Early attempts to hold ISPs legally responsible for the things their customers did were defeated when the law came to the conclusion that ISPs were simply *common carriers*, much like the telephone company, which also can't be held liable if someone uses the phone to commit an illegal act. The 1998 Digital Millennium Copyright Act permits that, so long as an ISP exercises no control over content, it can rest on the common carrier defense, and it can't be held responsible for its property's misuse by a few bad apples.

Similarly, if someone creates web technology that's designed for legitimate uses, and someone else comes along and, without the knowledge of the technology creator, uses it for an illegitimate purpose, the technology owner won't be deemed to have contributory liability. However, if the technology is designed to serve essentially no other function than to facilitate copyright infringement, the owner of that technology can be found guilty of contributory infringement. Such was the situation in the famous *A&M Records v. Napster* case. Napster's website practically became the poster child for those who cried *"Internet piracy!"* It was designed specifically to allow people to swap digitally recorded music, which it was argued Napster could reasonably have been expected to know would result in copyright infringement. There was virtually no other function to Napster's software, and so in 2001 its then current service suffered a virtual death sentence at the hands of the Ninth Circuit Court of Appeals.[51]

So what do you do if you discover that an unauthorized copy of your art has found its way onto someone else's website? Your most direct route, of course, is to demand the website owner remove the file. Many times, it's just a case of the person who runs the website not knowing what the rules are. Most people aren't deliberately trying to break the law.

If contacting the website owner doesn't result in a satisfactory resolution, you can demand the website's ISP take down or eliminate access to the infringing material. The Digital Millennium Copyright Act added a liability-free safe harbor for an ISP, which, assuming it had no knowledge of the infringing act, responds "expeditiously to remove, or disable access" once it has been notified. Therefore, if you give an ISP proper notice that your copyright is being infringed by someone using its web space, the ISP has a strong incentive to act reasonably quickly. Under Section 512(c) of the Copyright Act, your notification to an ISP must include:

- Your physical or electronic signature;
- Identification of the copyrighted work, or works, you're claiming have been infringed;
- Identification of the infringing material, and information reasonably sufficient to permit the service provider to locate that material;
- Information reasonably sufficient to permit the service provider to contact you, including, if available, an email address;
- A statement that you have a good faith belief that the use of the material on the website is not authorized by you (the copyright owner), your agent, or the law; and
- A statement that the information in the notification is accurate, and under penalty of perjury, that you are authorized to act on behalf of the owner (probably you) of an exclusive right that is allegedly infringed.

---

51 Napster was later reborn as a legal pay-for-music business.

If neither the infringer nor the ISP provides a satisfactory response to your complaint, then, as with any other form of copyright infringement, you have the litigation option. Of course, one of the more troubling things about the Internet is its "borderless" nature. It spills over into all segments of the globe. So infringing activity could occur virtually anywhere, and one country's cyber laws may not be the same as another's. However, thanks to copyright treaties, the long arm of the law can now reach far off lands, and international prosecutions of such things do take place. So, if you've got the willingness and money to prosecute, you might just be able to chase those Internet pirates across the Seven Seas.

Digital Rights Management

Ever since the day when cassette tapes replaced phonograph records as the era's recorded audio format of choice, and videotape recorders popped up in the homes of everyday people, the entertainment industry has had to live with the realization that people are making unauthorized copies of recorded music and videos to share with friends. These weren't necessarily pirates but, more often than not, just people who have a mindset that goes something like this:

I bought the recording. I own the recording. So I should be able to make a copy of the recording for a friend.

However, one has only so many friends with similar aesthetic taste, and copying songs or movies in real time from tape to tape is time consuming. So, in those earlier days, the entertainment industry begrudgingly accepted the unauthorized copying as a fact of life. (Okay, it accepted it after it lost a key court battle in which it tried unsuccessfully to put a stop to the sale of home video recorders.[52]) But, with the coming of the digital age, almost instantaneous copying, and worldwide distribution over the Internet, the problem for the industry has increased exponentially.

As with anything else where there's big money involved, people got busy and started to innovate. One innovation that has come onto the scene

---

52   That was the case of *Sony Corporation of America v. Universal City Studios*, which in 1984 went all the way to the United States Supreme Court and resulted in the High Court ruling that the sale of video cassette recorders did not constitute contributory infringement because they could also be used for non-infringing activities such as simply "time shifting" when a viewer would watch a show.

is something called *digital rights management*—or DRM, for short. For the benefit of the uninitiated, DRM is an electronic means of building into a digital product a code that prevents it from being reproduced, or, in the alternative, a code that scrambles the contents of the product if you try to play it on an unauthorized machine. Pop in a friend's DRM-protected DVD and try to burn a copy for yourself, and it just won't happen. The product protects itself from copyright infringement.

Think of it as techies standing guard at the castle gate, pulling up the drawbridge any time someone attempts to carry off a piece of the sovereign's property. If you're the sovereign, that might sound like a pretty good thing. As a copyright holder, an artist is something of a sovereign ruler over his own intellectual property, and the Copyright Act bestows fairly extensive, albeit not unlimited, rights to control what's done with your own creations. Therefore, digital rights management is the entertainment industry's answer to those who either don't understand or merely ignore those legal rights.

So what could possibly be objectionable about technology that simply helps enforce the law?...Well, plenty, if you listen to the arguments of various people who oppose DRM's growing encroachment into digital media. These aren't just people who desire to make unauthorized copies. They're also people who want just to be able to continue making the copies that the law *allows* them to make. Remember that Section 107 of the Copyright Act permits certain fair use exceptions to the copyright holder's exclusive rights. Excerpts of a copyrighted work can be copied for the purpose of such things as criticism, comment, news reporting, teaching, scholarship, and research. The trouble is that DRM technology can't distinguish between the legal and the illegal uses. It blocks them all equally.

Another thorny issue involves the use of DRM for the purpose of something known as *region coding*. That's where DRM is used to restrict which parts of the world can play the product. If, for example, you're using a machine built and sold in Europe, the region coding for a DVD purchased in the United States might not work in that European machine. My understanding is that this type of DRM is supposed to protect against digital works being smuggled into countries where they haven't yet been officially released for distribution or where the exclusive distribution rights for that part of the world belong to some other vendor. One of the issues this raises for the anti-DRM side is that there's nothing in copyright law that grants the copyright owner the right to tell you where you can and can't enjoy the product once you've paid the price and purchased it legally. It doesn't work that way for any other forms of intellectual property. For instance, you can't insist that I not read a book I've purchase in an airport once the plane I've boarded crosses into another country's airspace. So the question must be asked: Does region coding stake a claim to more protection than the law grants?

If the true purpose of DRM is not to stop perfectly legal activities but, rather, to combat the rising threat of bootleg distributions perpetrated by profit-motivated pirates—and that is often the case that's made for it—there still exists one truism that even the pro-DRM people are likely forced to admit: Build a better mousetrap, and there's bound to be a geeky mouse somewhere out there who's going to figure out a way to beat it. The real pirates stop at nothing to crack the codes designed to keep them out, and more than a few digital safeguards and firewalls have tumbled before the industrious hacker.

So whom then will DRM most likely, unfailingly keep from storming the castle? Naturally, the answer is *the rest of us*—the basically law-abiding, non-pirate, "not-makin'-a-nickel-on-it" folk who maybe just want to make a perfectly legal fair use copy but who'll be stopped dead in our tracks by a technology that forbids it. In an article I once wrote for an American Bar Association national institute on computing and the law, I compared this situation to one in which you install a piranha-filled moat around a cookie jar while leaving a maximum security prison guarded by a goldfish with a nasty disposition. It's overkill for the former and not nearly enough for the latter. But DRM is, at least as of this writing, still in its infancy. No doubt there will be some tweaking yet to come.

I also realize that, again as of the time of this writing, most artists aren't in any way engaged in the high tech practice of encoding digital rights management into their art. At the moment, that's more of a thing going on at the corporate level. However, it has been my experience that the out-of-reach technology of today quickly becomes the everyday appliance of tomorrow. Almost nobody had a computer in his home in the 1970s. Today the majority of Americans probably do. So I can readily imagine a day not far off when simple, solitary artists working out of garages and basements are employing DRM to protect their digitized intellectual property. Consider this a rudimentary primer for when that day arrives.

What Contracts Does the Artist Make?

Okay, now that you know what you own, what you're selling, what you can use, what you can't use, what you can say, what you can't say, and how to keep it all relatively safe, it's time to get down to the nitty-gritty of inking the deal. An artist who moves beyond the hobby stage is an artist who is probably going to be entering into legally enforceable contracts with others. That's the way business is done. This book makes not the slightest endeavor toward counseling creative people about the aesthetics of their art but, rather, attempts to arm them with enough legal knowledge to make them better businesspeople in their fields. Knowing your business as well as your craft is important to you as a professional. Legal acumen is by no means the only helpful skill in running a successful business. Production, marketing, managing, accounting, and handling taxes[53] are just a few other concerns of the well-prepared businessperson. But our focus in this book is the law, and nothing screams the word *"law"* like a *legal document*. A *contract* is a legal document. Let us examine then the types of contracts an artist might make in the course of doing business.

First, I present for your consideration that old quip—the one that adopts a bit of Yogi Berra-like logic—that goes: *An oral contract isn't worth the paper it's printed on.*

Now, for the record, generally speaking, oral contracts are legal and enforceable. There are some oral contracts that aren't enforceable under

---

53   Peter Jason Riley's book, *New Tax Guide for Writers, Artists, Performers, & Other Creative People* (Focus Publishing 2009), provides an easy-to-understand primer on income taxes as they relate to artists.

state laws—things such as transfers of real estate, sales the value of which is at least a certain amount (often five hundred dollars or more), and agreements that cannot under any circumstances be completed within one year. However, a simple oral contract, such as your accepting a friend's offer to give you a violin if you give her three-hundred dollars, is a perfectly legal and binding agreement between the two of you, despite the fact that there's nothing on paper memorializing the sale. If you turn over the three hundred bucks, and your friend doesn't give you the violin, that's a breach of contract.

The two obvious problems with an oral contract are:

- proving its existence, and,
- even if its existence isn't in question, proving the specific terms of the agreement should a dispute arise.

This is why you're not likely to find too many lawyers who'll advise you that it's okay to do business with oral contracts. When it comes to business, stick with paper.

"Oh, but, Rich," you cry, "surely I don't need a written contract if the agreement is just between a friend and me. We're pals. We trust each other."

Of course, you do. If you didn't, you wouldn't be doing business together. It's unlikely you'd even remain friends if you felt you couldn't trust the other person. But let's take a situation in which you and your good pal, Ken, engage in a little business venture. You've written this charming little children's story about a gopher who moves to the city to become a professional actor. And you've asked Ken, always the artsy one in the crowd, to draw some illustrations to go with the text. You tell Ken that, if the book gets published, you'll give him twenty-five percent of whatever you make on it. Ken agrees and draws a handful of sketches for you to include when you shop it around to publishers. The two of you don't bother with anything like a formal contract. After all, you and Ken are best pals. And signing a contract would be like saying you *don't trust each other.* Hey, c'mon! We're talkin' about good ol' Ken, here!

Well, lo and behold, a publisher snatches up the rights and publishes the book. You get your check and you give Ken his twenty-five percent, just like you said you would. Everyone's happy.

Then a few months pass, and you get a phone call from the publisher who's offering to pay you to make a sound recording of the text on an audio

CD version of the book. "Great!" you think to yourself. "Another check for me!"

"Great!" says Ken when you tell him about the CD. "Another check for me!"

"But, um…" you stammer with embarrassment, "it's just audio, Ken. They won't be using any of your drawings."

"So what?" reasons Ken. "You said I get twenty-five percent of whatever you make on it."

"That was twenty-five percent of whatever I make if the *book* gets published," you quickly add. "This isn't a printing of a book. It's an audio recording."

"So?"

"So your drawings don't have anything to do with audio."

"Whaddaya talkin' 'bout?! My drawings are what made the book a hit with the kids! It never would've got published without 'em! You *owe* me!"

Ah, it all started out so well. Everyone was a pal…until the money started coming in. That's when pals with the best intentions find out the hard way that their oral agreement has more holes in it that the proverbial Swiss cheese. In the above example, no one's really clear on what they agreed to. And, at this point, even if it all gets worked out in the end, there's a serious danger that the friendship with good ol' Ken will never be the same again. The trust that once existed between friends has been damaged.

This is why I strongly urge everyone to put all business agreements in writing and have that writing spell out the details of exactly what it is everyone's agreeing to. A formal contract may be overkill for many simple, uncomplicated matters of everyday life. But the specifics of any significant business venture (and I'm guessing your art is probably *significant* to you) ought to be committed to a signed written contract. That's in everyone's best interest.

In this chapter, I'm going to provide a brief overview of some basic elements of various types of contracts often entered into by artists. It in no way encompasses every potential agreement relevant to the arts and entertainment industries. Nor could I reasonably include that volume of information in a single book. There are just too many different possibilities. At best, the following examples are just some broad illustrations of general types of agreements covering an array of arts-related business situations. Since the following discussions are deliberately broad in nature, it's possible you might find a useful tidbit or two in any of them, even if the category doesn't

necessarily apply to you, personally. However, if one or more of these categories is completely irrelevant to what you do as an artist, you're welcome
to skip past them.

Furthermore, because every agreement is unique to its particular situation, it is impossible for any book to provide exact contract wording applicable to any and all similar circumstances. The contract language I provide
in this book is offered *only for illustration purposes* and cannot be plucked
verbatim from this text and pasted into a formal agreement with any assurance that it will serve the intended purpose of the parties to that agreement.
*Every contract must be drafted to the specifics of what has been negotiated
between the parties; a mere template of contract language may not, by itself,
be sufficient.*

As with everything else involving the law, if you don't feel confident
either drafting or interpreting an agreement onto which you're going to commit your signature, consult an attorney before you sign.

Collaborators

Some of the most basic and common work arrangements in the arts and
entertainment fields are those involving *collaborators*. The you-write-the-
lyrics-and-I'll-write-the-music type of agreement pervades the arts, possibly
at least in part because creative people are drawn to other creative people,
and sometimes just because several forms of artistic expression simply need
to incorporate the talents of more than one person. Unless you're the producer, director, and set/lighting designer of your own play, which also happens to be a one-person show starring you as the lone actor in it, chances are
you're going to have to work with others to mount a production of the show.
In such situations, the first thing you need to get straight is who's a collaborator and who isn't.

First, it should be understood that not everyone who assists an artist
is automatically that artist's collaborator. Additionally, not every collaboration results in a *partnership* or *joint venture*. Partnerships and joint ventures, from a legal standpoint, are formal business entities. A collaboration
agreement need only establish that two or more people will be working on
the same project, either in a unified, simultaneous effort or individually as
contributors. They don't need to form an official business entity to do that.
To clarify that a business entity is specifically not being formed, some collaboration agreements will include language such as:

By entering this agreement, the parties in no way form, nor shall it be construed that they are forming, a partnership or joint venture between them.

At least equally important, if not even more so, is the understanding that someone who assists an artist during the creation of a work does not automatically become a *joint author*. This is critically important in determining copyright ownership. A joint author has an equal ownership in all rights associated with the intellectual property—that is, the rights to control, duplicate, exploit, and share in the profits generated by it. Someone who is not a joint author does not share in those rights.

The Supreme Court established in the 19th century, when it ruled on the *Burrow-Giles* case (the one involving the photo of Oscar Wilde[54]), that the definition of the word "author," at least as it's used in the Constitution, is anyone to whom some creative work owes its origin. That definition doesn't limit designated *authorship* only to those who have literally *written* something. One can be an author or a joint author of a creative work even without writing so much as a single word. It's not about words; it's about creative contribution.

But does that mean that a person who gives an artist a suggestion, which the artist then incorporates into the work, has instantly transformed himself into that artist's joint author? This was the issue the in the 1991 case of *Childress v. Taylor*. Actor Clarice Taylor wanted to perform a play about the late comedienne Jackie "Moms" Mabley. The only problem was there was no such play in existence—or, at least, none that Ms. Taylor wanted to perform. She undertook to research "Moms" Mabley's life story and then enlisted playwright Alice Childress to write a play based on the research and suggestions Ms. Taylor provided. After the initial production, the two women had a falling out that resulted in a lawsuit in which Ms. Taylor claimed to be a joint author of the play. The Second Circuit Court of Appeals determined that Ms. Taylor was *not* a joint author of the work because there was no evidence to suggest that Ms. Childress had contemplated or would have accepted an arrangement in which the script she was writing was jointly authored. The court ruled that collaboration alone is insufficient to establish joint authorship, and that the conditions by which joint authorship is attained are, first, that the person claiming joint authorship must have contributed

---

54   See p. 8.

something that itself is copyrightable, and, second, that, during its creation, both parties must have entertained the concept that they were jointly authoring the work.

The *Childress* standard was applied three years later by the Seventh Circuit in the case of *Erickson v. Trinity Theatre*. Here the matter involved a situation in which actors in a drama had offered various suggestions that the playwright subsequently incorporated into the script's final draft. Citing *Childress*, the court ruled against the actors seeking joint author status. During the creative process, there was no explicit understanding that the actors would be the playwright's joint authors. Therefore, they weren't.

Editors, script doctors, dramaturgs, and the like are not joint authors simply because someone has brought one of them in to offer assistance. However, the waters got a bit murky when the Second Circuit Court of Appeals ruled in 1998 on the case of *Thomson v. Larson*. That much publicized case involved a dispute over the hit Broadway musical, *Rent*. After its author, Jonathan Larson, died, Lynn Thomson, whom the theater had hired to help Mr. Larson punch up his script, sued the Larson estate, claiming that she was the author of key elements of the show. Although a pleading technicality resulted in the case ending with a ruling against Ms. Thomson, the court suggested in its published opinion that a non-author might retain independent copyright interests in certain parts that the non-author specifically contributed to the work. The suggestion that someone might have the right to extract his own contributions sent shivers down the spine of many playwrights and other artists who envisioned the gory nightmare of seeing their works disemboweled of key components by people who had helped them during the creative process.

To the best of my knowledge, that sort of artistic dismemberment hasn't occurred in any newsworthy example. However, artists on both sides of such issues need to be aware of the possibilities that may be lurking out there. If it's your expectation that you're going to be a joint author for your contributions to the creation of a work—or if it's your desire that you absolutely *not* have a joint author foist upon you by someone who offers to pair you up with somebody who can lend a helping hand—this is not the sort of thing you want to leave to the vagaries of a handshake deal. Get it down on paper and get it signed *before* beginning the collaboration.

When joint authorship is the goal, one of the most important things that should be determined in the agreement is the issue of *merger*. I'm not talking about the sort of merger that occurs when one corporation merges with another to form an even bigger corporation. Rather, the merger that applies to collaborative creations is one in which all the individual contributions are merged into a single, indivisible work. Prior to merger taking place, each collaborator is legally capable of removing his own contributions and retaining his own separate copyright in those contributions. If, for example, people are collaborating on a new musical, and the choreographer leaves the show (by choice or otherwise) prior to merger taking place, the choreographer could now insist the producers take his dance steps out of the show, and the choreographer could then re-use that choreography elsewhere. In this case, the exclusive rights to those steps never left the possession of the choreographer. However, once merger has taken place, there's no going back. At that point, the legally divisible individuality of contributions ceases to exist, and a contributor cannot remove the bits and pieces he created from the merged work as a whole. From a legal standpoint, that's the stage at which all elements have merged as one, and all of the work's authors share in the copyright ownership of the total work—that is, those parts each author created himself as well as those parts his co-authors created.

Contractually, merger can take place at any point in the creative process. A collaboration agreement can include a clause that specifies exactly when merger takes place. For, let's say, a literary work, publication or final submission to the publisher could be the triggering event for merger. In the performing arts, sometimes it's the first paid performance or the official opening at a particular venue that triggers it. It's possible that multiple, various occurrences might trigger merger or, in the alternative, the pre-merger termination of the agreement. There might, for example, be contract language such as:

> *The parties agree that all rights of every kind and nature in the work shall be merged for all purposes upon the soonest of the following occurring:*
>
> *(a) publication of the work;*
>
> *(b) the first paid performance of the work;*
>
> *(c) three years following the execution date of this agreement.*
>
> *No merger shall apply to any contributions that have been deleted prior to merger. In the event that there is no merger*

within _____ years from the execution date of this agreement, any party to this agreement shall have the right, upon written notice to the others, to terminate this agreement, and all rights in the work shall revert in full to the respective copyright owner free and clear of any rights or claims of the other parties to this agreement.

Other key elements of a collaboration agreement could determine such things as attribution credits, proportionate shares of proceeds, what happens in the event of a collaborator's death, and the process by which decisions about the work are to be made. As you might imagine, even the best of friends might disagree as to how a joint work should be marketed or otherwise exploited. There might be further disagreements regarding necessary changes or alterations to the work. Having an early agreement over how to handle such situations is a way to avoid a later stalemate. A sample of contractual language that deals with such things might look like this:

Wherever approval or consent of the author of the work is required, each party comprising the author of the work shall have one vote, and a majority of such votes will be controlling. If there is a tie vote, all of the parties to this agreement agree to submit the matter to arbitration in the state of _____ in accordance with the Commercial Arbitration Rules of the American Arbitration Association. Judgment upon the award rendered by the arbitrator may be entered in any court having jurisdiction thereof.

Yes, I do realize that all this legalese has a way of taking a noble and passionate endeavor such as art and making it sound like a cold and heartless business. But, if you take care of all that nasty business stuff at the very start, so that we all know exactly where we stand and what we can expect, then you can turn with confidence to your fellow collaborator and say—just as Humphrey Bogart did in *Casablanca*—"I think this is the beginning of a beautiful friendship."

Visual Art or Design Purchasers

Unless a visual artist is a staff employee of whoever buys the works that artist creates, much of the paying work a visual artist gets comes in the form of commissions. The buyer agrees to compensate the artist (usually with money) in return for the artist creating a particular piece that meets the buyer's needs or desires.

Note what I said: a commission is a contract that's typically geared toward the *buyer's* needs or desires. When the artist accepts a commission, it's either explicitly or implicitly understood that the artist will adhere to the buyer's wishes. Perhaps it's not what Adrienne dreamed of when she was attending art school, but, when Arthur offered her a thousand dollars to paint a portrait of his hamster, Adrienne bit her lip as she accepted and thought to herself, "What the heck—it's a paying gig." So long as she provides Arthur a portrait of his hamster, Adrienne has fulfilled her part of the contract. If she chooses to substitute some other portrait—even one that might be considerably more valuable—she will be guilty of breaching the contract and will be subject to whatever legal recourse is available to Arthur. I recognize that many artists find it distasteful for non-artists to dictate what their art ought to be. But a contract that specifies the work will be a portrait of a hamster is not fulfilled by a portrait of an iguana. Artistic license only goes so far.

To avoid potential troubles or misunderstandings, it's important that commissioning agreements spell out certain ground rules. For instance, does the commission specify the subject matter of the art, or is the subject matter something left up to the artist to decide? Does it specify the artistic style or motif (e.g., naturalistic, impressionistic, abstract)? Does it specify the medium or materials (e.g., oil painting, watercolors, charcoal drawing)? Depending on the notoriety of the artist, some art commissioners might be happy with almost any original work by that artist, or perhaps the commissioners will accept any work by that artist so long as it adheres to a certain form or genre (e.g., any landscape). From the artist's perspective, the fewer particularities in the commissioning agreement, the better—not merely from an artistic standpoint but also from a contractual one. Fewer specifications are fewer things to get tripped up on, especially where certain definitions might be subject to personal interpretation. You don't want to go through all the time and trouble of sculpting the classic nude, "The Thinker," only to have the buyer show up on the delivery date and say, "But the commissioning agreement explicitly says no indecent images!" (Recall that imprecise "I know it when I see it" definition of obscenity?) If the commissioning party has specific notions about what the art must or must not contain, then the artist, as a personal safeguard, should make certain they both have the same sense of what it is they're talking about. Remember, a legal battle over an artistic commission will hinge on whether the parties lived up to their end of the bargain *as specified in the contract.*

Graphic designers—the people who create illustrations, logos, visual designs, and the like—are sometimes regular employees of large consumers of such graphics. However, because the need for that type of work happens on a more sporadic frequency for most smaller buyers, graphic artists are often independent contractors who sell their services on a per assignment basis. Each of those assignments requires a separate agreement between artist and buyer.

As you may recall, an independent contractor doesn't automatically relinquish with the sale of art the ownership of the copyright attached to that art. That remains the independent artist's possession unless it's specifically transferred to another. Buyers relying on their ability to re-use graphic elements again and again are understandably disinclined to have to renegotiate their purchase of those graphics every time a new utilization opportunity arises. For that reason, a buyer might insist that a graphic design agreement include language such as:

> *The Artist hereby assigns to the Buyer, its successors and assigns, the Artist's entire right, title, and interest in and to the copyrights to all original, creative works created for the Buyer pursuant to this agreement. The term "creative works" includes, but is not limited to, artwork, graphics, designs, logos, sketches, drawings, illustrations, photographs, text, fonts, and accompanying writings.*

In the alternative, the contract language might say:

> *The Artist understands and agrees that all original, creative works created for the Buyer pursuant to this agreement shall be considered "works made for hire," and the Buyer shall be the owner of all rights, title, and interest in and to the copyrights to such work.*

As discussed in an earlier chapter, a "work made for hire" is automatically the intellectual property of the buyer and requires no separate transfer of copyright ownership. If it's not your intention to give away the copyright on your work, do not sign a contract that declares what you're creating for the buyer to be a work made for hire. Once the copyright belongs to someone else, you, the artist, can no longer legally utilize that work in any way without the copyright owner's permission. Quite simply, the work doesn't belong to you.

Even in those cases where an artist must give away the copyright to the buyer, it may still be possible for the artist to retain certain rights for non-competing uses. For example, if a literary publisher hires you to shoot some photos for a book, that publisher will probably insist that those photos not turn up in someone else's competing book. However, the publisher might have no objection whatsoever to you displaying the photographs in a gallery or museum; or the publisher might have no objection to you including those photos in your own professional portfolio that you show to potential clients. Neither of those uses would be likely in any way to negatively impact the sale of the book. So, to retain those non-competing rights, you might include in the agreement language saying something like:

Notwithstanding any other provisions in this agreement, the Artist reserves the right to utilize the works created pursuant to this agreement in non-competing uses, including, but not limited to, public displays and professional portfolios.

If you're intending to reserve certain rights in a copyright transfer, I recommend that you agree to *assign the copyright* to the buyer (that is, sell it to the buyer) rather than create the art as a work made for hire. As we've noted, a work made for hire belongs lock, stock, and barrel to the buyer, who would then technically be required to transfer to you any rights you desire to have. If it's not a work made for hire, you, as the artist, can transfer to the buyer only those rights you intend to part with while never relinquishing the rights you intend to keep. Practically speaking, the end result might be exactly the same. But, as a lawyer representing the artist, I'd just feel more comfortable arguing in court that the buyer possessed only those rights expressly transferred by contract and never had any claim of ownership on the rights my client expressly reserved.

Literary Publishers

Literary publishing rights can either be assigned (that is, sold outright) or licensed (in which the license grants the publisher the right to engage in certain pursuits involving the literary property without actually transferring ownership of those rights from the author to the publisher). The major difference between an assigned right and a licensed one is that a license can have an expiration date after which the licensed rights cease and the publisher must either discontinue its exploitation of the literary property or negotiate a new contract.

In either case, an author entering into a publishing contact will likely have to grant the publisher the ability to print, publish, distribute, sell, and generally exploit the work in at least one if not more formats or media. Once, the publishing industry had basically two general formats with which people concerned themselves—hardcover and paperback. Now, thanks to technological advances, there are various other ways in which books and other literature are published. These days literature is being distributed through such things as electronic books, online databases, and interactive and multi-media systems. Often publishers will exploit a work by featuring it in more than one of these formats. Additionally, *publishing-on-demand,* in which literature is stored in electronic format and a printed copy made only upon purchase by the consumer, has been a growing trend in the publishing industry. All of these options might turn up in a publishing contract, as well as a clause addressing the publisher's rights regarding "like media and technologies, whether now known or hereafter devised." In other words, if someone invents it and it can be used to make a buck on your book, you can bet the publisher wants a piece of it, and it'll probably be addressed in the publishing contract.

Key elements of a basic publishing contract are likely to include such things as the author's deadlines, the publisher's timeline for publication, costs, rights for the work to be published in particular media, distribution rights worldwide or in a specified region, and, of course, the author's compensation.

There's no one absolute rule as regards the compensation an author earns from a literary work. A lot depends on the notoriety or marketability of the author, and an awful lot depends on the size of the publisher. Advances, for example, might be nominal or nonexistent when dealing with smaller publishers, or they could be several thousand dollars if you sell a book to one of the big publishing houses. A typical advance clause might read something like:

> *The Publisher shall pay to the Author, as an advance against royalties and any other amounts owing by the Publisher to the*

Author under this agreement, the sum of $_____ to be paid as follows: one-third upon the signing of this agreement, one-third upon the delivery and acceptance of the complete manuscript, and one-third upon the publication of the work in the first publisher's edition.

An advance, as the term suggests, is an *advance against future royalties* earned by the author. The publisher will deduct that amount from any royalties due the author until the advance has been fully deducted. Only then, assuming the author isn't responsible for any additional costs, will the author begin to earn additional compensation through royalties. A publishing contract might also impose costs on an author for certain expenses the publisher incurs for things such as indexing and accompanying art created by outside third parties. A wary author might want to include in the agreement a clause that states such costs won't exceed a certain dollar limit without the author's prior approval.

The method by which royalties are calculated is an important element of any publishing contract in which royalties are to be paid to the author. Generally speaking, the industry standard for book royalties is about:

- Hardcover = 10 – 15%
- Trade softcover = 7 – 10%
- Mass market paperback = 6 – 8%

The question, of course, is: what is that royalty percentage a percentage *of*? Often it's a percentage of what the industry calls the "invoice price" on "net copies sold." The *invoice price* is defined as the price shown on the publisher's invoices to wholesalers and retailers, and it's that price from which the publisher's discounts to those buyers are calculated. The difference between the invoice price and the suggested retail price is typically no more than five percent. Meanwhile, *net copies sold* is defined as sales of the book less returns of any copies sold by the publisher through conventional channels of distribution in the book trade. When negotiating a publishing contract that uses these terms, it's always best to have the contract include a clause that defines them so that there's no disagreement later over what was actually meant.

There's no rule that says royalties have to be based on the invoice price. Some publishing agreements base royalties on a percentage of the net revenues a publisher derives from the sale of the work. Here, again, it's important to define in such a contract what's meant by the term "net revenues."

A standard definition might be that it refers to money actually received by the publisher from the sale of copies of the work after deducting the costs of shipping, insurance, commissions, fees, collections, customs, and currency exchange.

It's also possible to contract for royalties to be paid on an escalating basis. If, let's say, a book becomes a runaway best seller, the author might feel shortchanged by a small percentage royalty that doesn't reflect what the author believes is an accurate value of his work. To guard against such things, the royalties percentages might be scaled to the number of copies that are sold. For example, the contract might read:

> *For each edition of the work the Publisher publishes under this agreement, the Publisher shall credit the Author's account with the following royalties:*
>
> *(1) 10% of the invoice price on the first 10,000 net copies sold;*
>
> *(2) 12.5% of the invoice price on the next 10,000 net copies sold;*
>
> *(3) 15% of the invoice price on sales in excess of 20,000 net copies sold.*

The publisher might insist that the contract language be further defined to say that the "net copies sold" criterion applies to any one *edition*, which could be defined as the published work in any particular content, format, and length that has not been materially revised or redesigned. A significant revision to the way the text is packaged, and presented would constitute a new edition that would start the counter over at zero in calculating escalating royalties for that particular edition.

Because published literary works can have a life beyond their original written format, a publishing agreement should also address revenues derived from licensed rights granted to third parties, sometimes called *subsidiary rights*. These licenses could include the rights to such things as: book clubs; periodical publication; translations; foreign distributions; microfilm/microfiche; readings; audio recordings; dramatic performances; motion pictures; television; radio; and commercials; as well as the electronic and future technologies mentioned earlier. Something called a "flow-through clause" (even if it's not labeled as such in the contract) should state that the author's share of any revenues the publisher derives from the exploitation of third-party licenses will be paid to the author by the publisher within a set period of time (such as within thirty days after receipt by the publisher), and the standard division of such revenues is often a 50/50 split between the publisher and the author. As with any agreement, the parties to the contract are free to tinker with the details of such third-party licensing clauses, including the author's percentage cut of revenues and whether or not a particular licensing right is being reserved exclusively by the author. Naturally, authors with greater clout are likely to be able to negotiate more favorable deals for themselves. That's just the way of the world, my friends. Write that best seller, and you, too, might become one of those clout-wielding authors.

Among the other elements of a publishing agreement that are important to the author are those that make provisions for *editing, revision,* and *acceptance.* Authors are generally protective of their work and fearful of what could happen if someone else takes an editor's pen to their words. As a safeguard relating to such things, authors will often negotiate into a publishing contract a clause that says something like:

> *No changes shall be made to the text of the manuscript without the author's prior written consent, except for routine copyediting and correction of grammar and spelling.*

If the publisher rejects the submitted manuscript because of some editorial deficiencies, the author typically would like the opportunity to cure those deficiencies prior to a full-scale rejection and termination of the publishing contract. This can be achieved by including a clause to the effect that the author will have the opportunity to generally revise, correct, and/or supplement the work to the publisher's satisfaction within a certain period of time. Additionally, because an author doesn't want to be left hanging for a veritable eternity awaiting the publisher's decision as to whether the work has been accepted, it's also a good idea to have a clause which states that the work will be deemed accepted by the publisher for all purposes unless rejected in writing within a certain number of days.

Another key clause, and one that is sometimes the subject of much negotiation, involves *options.* Publishers often require that, in consideration of their efforts to publish your literary work, they be given the option of having first crack at publishing your next work *on the same terms and conditions of the first publishing contract.* If you'll note the phrase that I've italicized, you can probably readily understand why authors aren't too crazy about having this provision in their publishing agreements. While it's nice to be wanted, an author whose first work rockets him to the top of the best seller list might feel it unfair for him to be legally obligated to sell his next work for the same paltry sum he agreed to on the first work when he was an unknown. What's more, the *same terms* would likely also include the *same option clause* that would again require the author to give the publisher the option to publish yet *another work* without any augmented compensation to the author. However, if you're in a position where you feel you have no choice but to agree to such an option, there are some things you might try to negotiate into the clause to help lessen its impact. For example, the option clause could be drafted to specify that it applies just to a certain category of your work, such as your "next work of science fiction only." Additionally, to break the cycle of never-ending option clauses that mandate the same terms over and over, you could have the clause drafted such that it states something like:

> *The Publisher shall have the option to publish the Author's next work on the same terms and conditions set forth in this agreement except that the contract for publication of the Author's next work shall not include an option of any kind in favor of the Publisher regarding any of the Author's subsequent work.*

With this type of language, the author's on the hook to honor the option just once, and then he's free to negotiate new deals with either the same or different publishers for any later works he produces.

At some point after the contract is signed and the manuscript has been accepted, the author will probably want to see his work either get published or, in the alternative, get returned to him so he can seek another publisher. No one likes to sit around forever waiting to find out whether or not something is going to happen. (It's the old "you-know-what or get off the pot" philosophy.) There ought to be something that protects an author from the purgatory of publishing limbo. There is. It's called a *reversion clause.* Such a clause should be drafted to specify that, once the final delivered manuscript has been accepted, there is a certain time limit (perhaps twelve to twenty-four months) in which the book must finally hit the streets for sale. The clause should state that, if the publisher fails to do that, all rights in the work will wholly and automatically revert to the author, who is then free to take it to another publisher without any obligation to the original publisher.

Furthermore, even after publication, an author might still want to reclaim the rights to a literary work that has gone out of print or that has failed to perform commercially to a certain level. A reversion clause could dictate the situations by which all rights in the work revert to the author. Work that clause into the contract and, if the book is underperforming with one publisher, you can try your luck with it elsewhere.

Music Publishers

In some ways, music publishing deals are similar to literary publishing deals. For instance, the songwriter can either sell outright or license for a limited time to the publisher the music he has written. Contract provisions in a music publishing agreement can include familiar elements such as advances, costs, royalties, options, reversions, the publisher's role in the marketing and distribution, and the like. However, the music industry is a special breed of animal that often defies even insiders' attempts at fully understanding the intricacies of how it all works. I'll tell you, here and now, that you're not going to become an authority on the legal aspects of the music industry simply by reading this book. Whole volumes and treatises have been devoted to the topic, and oftentimes even the experts seem to shrug when attempting to expound exactitudes regarding the music biz. My purpose, then, in writing this section of this chapter is, as it has been for the entire book, to impart just some basic legal concepts and knowledge to those who have no formal background in such areas. I'll touch on a few key points I feel you, the artist, should be aware of, and then I'll leave you with the best advice I can offer: When in doubt about the legal ramifications of a contract you're asked to sign, don't guess. Consult a lawyer. (Yes, I know I sound like the proverbial broken record repeating that over and over. But the biggest legal problems, and the ones that are so often costly to fix, frequently result from the acts of non-lawyers thinking they can save a few bucks by handling all the legal stuff themselves.)

The first thing the songwriter should determine about a music publishing contract is whether it's an *exclusive* or a *non-exclusive* agreement. Non-exclusive agreements involve the sale of a particular piece or pieces of music. Let's say Frank has written a song that Rinky-Dink Music Publishers wishes to publish. The non-exclusive contract specifies exactly which song is being acquired by the publishers, and Frank's free to sell any other songs he writes to anyone else. On the other hand, an exclusive music publishing agreement binds the songwriter's services exclusively to that publisher, and all songs written by the writer during the term of the contract automatically become the property of the publisher. Exclusive contracts typically include a minimum commitment—that is, the number of songs the songwriter must write for the publisher within a given period of time (usually somewhere in the neighborhood of about fifteen per year). These exclusive publishing arrangements are sometimes drafted such that they designate the songs as *works made for hire* or the songwriter as an *employee* of the publisher, which amounts to the same thing as far as copyright is concerned. A songwriting employee acting within the scope of his employment, or an independent contractor who has agreed in writing to make his songs a work made for hire, will never be deemed to have been the copyright owner of those compositions. If Frank is Rinky-Dink's songwriting employee, the songs he writes for it will forever belong to Rinky-Dink, even if Frank later leaves that publisher's employ.

Regardless of who will own the copyright, the standard music publishing contract makes provisions for the songwriter to receive compensation for the full term of the copyright. That compensation can take the form of various types of royalties. Potentially the most lucrative of these is what's called *mechanical license fees*, often just referred to as "mechanicals." This is the fee recording companies must pay the copyright holder in order to make the song into a recording that will be sold to the public. The statutory royalty rate for mechanicals, which has been inching up from two cents back in 1978, was raised in 2006, for songs running five minutes or less, from 8.5 cents to 9.1 cents per recorded copy. (That same year, the rate for songs over five minutes long was raised from 1.65 to 1.75 cents per minute or fraction thereof. E.g., a song with a running time between five-minutes-and-one-second and six minutes would be calculated as: 6 minutes x \$.0175 = 10.5¢.)

The second most lucrative fee for the songwriter is probably the *public performance fee*. This is the fee collected by performing rights societies like ASCAP, BMI, and SESAC, and they are the fees paid to the songwriter and publisher for the right to perform the song publicly. That includes live performances before audiences, piped in recorded music at stores, restaurants, and the like, and broadcasts on radio and television. These are referred to as the song's *small performance rights* (as compared to the *grand performance rights*, both of which were covered in the third chapter's discussion of music rights).

Then there are also *synchronization license fees*. The "sync" license is necessary whenever someone puts music to visual images such as a motion picture or a video. The license is required regardless of whether the music was recorded originally for the visuals or comes from some preexisting recording. And, no, this license doesn't only apply where the images are visually in sync with the melody or the beat of the song. It's not that kind of synchronization the license is referring to.

Additionally, we can't forget the *print rights* to a piece of music. We're talking about sheet music, folios, lyric sheets included inside boxed CDs, and such. Basically, any reproduction in printed format would fall into the print rights category, and the author of the music is entitled to be compensated for it.

Finally, there could also be some special uses for a song (e.g., karaoke, video games, ringtones). A *special use* or "catch-all" clause in a music publishing contract typically encompasses the songwriter's desire to make sure nothing falls through the cracks. The contract language might look something like:

> *For any net income received by the Publisher, which is not provided for in any of the above paragraphs and for which the Songwriter does not receive direct payment of what has been termed the "writer's share," the Publisher shall pay the Songwriter fifty percent (50%) of such net income.*

The standard split for most of the above rights is one where fifty percent goes to the publisher and fifty percent to the songwriter. (For some reason, the standard compensation to the author for published sheet music sales is only about eight to twelve cents per copy. And, if you've priced sheet music anytime recently, you know that's nowhere near fifty percent of the retail price.) If a recording of your song goes gold or platinum, you can start doing the math yourself as to what that might translate into financially. However, often the statutory rate for mechanicals is negotiated downward by the big record labels that possess the clout to do so, and the songwriter's share of various proceeds could also get whittled down by administration fees or other costs for which the songwriter is responsible. So don't start pricing that yacht just yet.

In some instances, a music publisher will offer to co-publish a song-writer's music. This often happens in conjunction with recording contracts in which the record label's publisher subsidiary will be doing the publishing. Profits are divided proportionally between co-publishers. However, so are the costs involved in publishing the music. If Frank and Rinky-Dink are equal co-publishers of Frank's music, fifty cents of every dollar earned would be earned by each of them. But if Rinky-Dink expended costs for publishing, promoting, and generally exploiting the music that amounted to forty cents on every dollar, that would be forty cents Rinky-Dink would take off the top. The split between Frank and Rinky-Dink would then be thirty cents each, half of the remaining sixty cents. What's more, if there was a ten percent administration charge (and Rinky-Dink might insist it be the administrator of the copyright), that would be another dime taken off, leaving only fifty cents to be split in half, with Frank getting a sum of only twenty-five cents on the dollar. Additionally, if the co-publishing agreement designates that the copyright will be owned equally by the publisher, by you (the co-publisher), *and by the record label* (with whom you have a recording contract), there's a good chance that it might also say that the net proceeds are to be divided equally among the copyright holders. That would reduce Frank's share from one-half to one-third (in our example, leaving Frank with sixteen-and-two-thirds cents on the dollar).

Another thing to note carefully if entering into such an agreement is whether you're actually entering a co-publishing agreement or a *participation agreement*. While there may be no difference between them as far as sharing revenues is concerned, there's a big difference regarding ownership. A participation agreement implies that the participant does not own a share of the copyright. If Frank is simply a participant in the agreement, he's entitled to whatever share of compensation the contract designates, but he gives up any copyright control privileges.

Recording Companies

It used to be that there were basically two distinct types of artists involved in the making of a music recording—the artists who wrote the songs and the artists who performed them. While there were notable exceptions to this general rule, those exceptions were few and far between. For the most part, either you were Frank Sinatra or you were Cole Porter. It's not that Cole Porter never sang his own compositions in public. But, overwhelmingly, he left it to Ol' Blue Eyes and other recording stars of the day to make the songs famous with the general public.

Then came the 1960s, and, with the growing prominence of composing/performing groups like the Beatles, things in the industry began to shift away from the *either/or* specialization that had predominated earlier eras. More and more, the performers were writing their own music. For this reason, music publishing and recording industries have blurred the line to the point where a single contract often involves both the publishing and the recording aspects of the business. Even so, publishing and recording are two different elements of the music industry, and, therefore, for clarity, it's probably best to tackle our discussions of each separately. Hence, this section of the chapter will be devoted to agreements specifically for recording artists.

Unlike music publishing agreements, which can be either exclusive or non-exclusive, recording contracts are almost always exclusive agreements. The recording company binds the artist to that label—and that label only—for the term of the contract. The term is typically set for a period of time followed by various options for the company to extend it, if it so chooses. A sample of just such a clause in a recording contract might look like:

> *The Company engages the Artist's services as a vocalist and musician for the purpose of producing musical recordings for an initial period of one (1) year (the "Initial Contract Period") commencing upon the date of execution of this agreement. The Artist grants to the Company three (3) additional, consecutive options, each to renew this agreement for a Period of one (1) year beginning at the expiration of the immediately preceding Contract Period.*

There's nothing special about the *one-plus-three* numbers used in the above sample. The options could be fewer or more, and the time duration of each could be reduced or extended. Additionally, the contract could be for a flat term with no options. It's up to the contracting parties to negotiate the specifics. Regardless of how it's structured, though, the industry standard is that the contract, including all options, usually doesn't extend the term of the agreement beyond five years, and they almost never go more than seven years. That may be because California, through which almost all of the entertainment industry passes at some point, doesn't enforce *personal service contracts* beyond a seven-year period.[55] The definition of the term "personal service contract" includes the services a recording artist performs for a recording company.

Like the publishing deal, a recording contract is likely to have a minimum commitment clause. That is, it will specify the number of "masters" the artist is expected to record over a given period of time. A master, as it's typically defined, is a single song selection. (Terms such as "sides" and "cuts" are fairly anachronistic variations on the same terminology. In a world where music is now rarely found on the side of, or cut into, a phonograph record, if those terms are used in the agreement, it might benefit the understanding of both parties to have specific definitions built into the contractual language.) Regardless of the terminology used, be careful of contracts that specify a *minimum* number of masters but contain no *maximum*. You don't want to be in a position where the record company keeps demanding more and more and ends up stockpiling your music under the terms of an early contract where your compensation might be relatively slim.

Speaking of compensation…what would a recording contract be without a section detailing how much money the artist is to get in the form of advances or royalties?

People in the know will tell new recording artists that they should attempt to get as much money in the form of advances as they can because— and this is the stinging reality of the music business—it's likely to be the only money they ever see from the recording. The reason is that there are tremendous costs involved in manufacturing and marketing recordings, and the standard record contract makes the artist financially responsible for those costs, which will be deducted from any future royalties owed to the artist. The standard royalty rate for recording artists is about six to ten percent of the suggested retail price. From that money will be deducted the advance, of course, along with the costs of such things as the studio time, equipment rental, outside musicians or vocalists, engineers, arrangers, mixing, and mastering. Then there's also the *container charge*. This refers to the packaging in which the recording is housed for its marketing. When calculating the royalty payment, recording companies deduct up to 25 percent off the retail price as the container charge.

---

55   California Labor Code § 2855.

And then there's the bad boy of music contract language. The sinister presence lurking in the fine print. The Boris Badenov of cost accounting clauses.... I'm talking about a little something known as *cross-collateralization*.

Here, take a look at this language from a sample recording contract:

> *In consideration of the Artist's services and the related rights granted hereunder, the Company will pay the Artist a royalty of 10 (ten) percent of the royalties actually earned and received by the Company from its direct sale of the Artist's recordings, less any unrecouped advances, costs, and expenses chargeable against the Artist hereunder or under any other agreement between the Artist and the Company, on a semi-annual basis within sixty days of June 30th and December 31st of each year.*

Did you catch it? Were you able to spot the little devil in the details? Don't feel bad if you didn't. Contract language like this is designed to make the demons as unobtrusive as possible, and, unless you know what it is you're looking for, you could read that clause a hundred times and never fully realize what the key phrase is or what it actually means.

The key phrase, in this case, is *"or under any other agreement."* Why is that the key? Because what that's saying is that the record company can deduct all the many expenses I've already listed—and then some I didn't mention—not only from any royalties you're due from the sale of a recording made under this contract but, also, from the monies you're due under *any other contract* it has with you. In other words, if one of your albums loses money, but another of your albums is a big hit that makes money, the company can deduct from the royalties you're owned on the hit album money to cover the losses on the other album. What's more, if you're a performer/songwriter who has both a recording contract with a record label and also a publishing contract with its publishing branch, the company can siphon off the money you would have received from the publishing contract and use it to offset the costs incurred under the recording contract.

Think about our songwriter, Frank, who maybe also had a record deal with the company. Although Frank's album lost money, he's been consoling himself with the notion that at least he'll be getting a royalty check for the publishing of his one song that was a big hit. Then imagine the expression on Frank's face when he gets his semi-annual accounting statement from the company, and it says all his publishing royalties went bye-bye because they were used to recoup the losses on the totally separate recording contract that involved the money-losing album. Someone better make sure Frank isn't around any sharp instruments when he gets that statement.

Don't expect to see the term "cross-collateralization" actually printed in any recording contract. You're unlikely to find it. However, you can bet there's an excellent chance the clause is in there, worded with phrases such as "or under any other agreement," as was the case in our above example, or sometimes using wording that describes all agreements as being "deemed to be one accounting unit" or "a single accounting unit." It's unlikely a recording artist will be able to eliminate all cross-collateralization from the contract, but it might be possible to negotiate some limiting language. For example:

> *Notwithstanding anything to the contrary herein, the Company agrees that there shall be no cross-collateralization between the Artist's royalties due to the Artist pursuant to the recording agreement between the Artist and the Company and the Artist's royalties due to the Artist as a songwriter pursuant to the publishing agreement between the Artist and the Company.*

Or, in the alternative:

> *Notwithstanding anything to the contrary herein, the Company and the Artist expressly agree that the publishing agreement between the Artist and the Company shall be treated as a separate accounting unit from the recording agreement between the Artist and the Company and that no cross-collateralization shall occur between the two separate accounting units.*

With so many deductions in the recording end of the business, it's not impossible for the deductions to exceed the total of whatever royalties are due the artist. For this reason, and to be certain the artist doesn't end up getting a bill for the return of advance money, I recommend that the artist negotiate a contract clause that states the advance is *recoupable but nonrefundable*. It's bad enough that you're probably not ever going to see another penny from the contract. You sure don't want to have to send any back.

A final thought on the music industry... As rough businesses go, the recording industry is probably one of the roughest. For the reasons outlined above, and a whole bunch of reasons I haven't even touched on, even big-name stars sometimes can't turn a recording contract into a truly lucrative venture. At best, releasing a recording helps to get the music out to the public, and that can help boost a career for a music artist who picks up concert gigs and various types of promotional opportunities from which some real money can be made. If you're looking for a recording contract to make you wealthy, you might be very disappointed. However, if you negotiate the contract such that it could provide a substantial career boost, you never know where it might lead.

Agents and Managers

Comedian Jackie Vernon used to do a routine in which he'd narrate an imaginary slide show of a safari vacation in which he was being led by his guide around dangerous quicksand. The next slide was a picture of the guide from the waist up. Then a slide of the guide from the neck up. Finally, a slide of just the guide's hat.

The only reason I bring up this old, comic bit is to give me a little metaphor by which to launch into a brief discussion of the people who are professional "guides," so to speak, for the creative folks in the arts and entertainment industries—the people who know the jungles well and can lead a newcomer around the quicksand that could otherwise suck a promising career into oblivion. Of course, I'm talking about the agents and managers of artistic people. In some ways, the industry wouldn't exist without these agents and managers. They can open doors most artists couldn't even find to knock on, and many of the larger consumers of the arts—the corporate entities that sign the big contracts—won't even talk to an artist unless the pitch comes from an industry recognized representative. For this reason, many, if not most, professional artists who want to "crack the big time" find themselves sooner or later in the market for professional representation. This presents yet another contracting opportunity for the artist. So let's examine those types of agreements a little.

First, managers and agents are not one and the same. A personal manager's job is basically to help develop and promote the artist such that the artist becomes a more marketable commodity. An agent, by contrast, is someone who works professionally at seeking employment opportunities for the artist. In California, one needs to be licensed to be an agent, whereas, no license is necessary for a personal manager. It's possible for one to be both a manager and an agent. However, when signing an exclusive contract with one of these professionals (and these are almost always going to be *exclusive* agreements), it's important for the artist to know exactly what services are being contracted.

With someone who is exclusively an agent, it's pretty straightforward. The deal is that the agent will attempt to find you work, and you'll pay the agent a percentage commission (usually between 10 and 15 percent) on the money you earn from those jobs. On the other hand, a manager earns his money by providing advice, counsel, and guidance on such things as how to market your work, how to generate publicity, how to reflect the appropriate public image, how to select the most advantageous artistic choices, and, if you're in the performing arts, how to dress and present yourself visually. Even if the manager is not acting as an agent, it's typical that the manager will also want to review all employment engagements before they're finalized to ensure that they're good career moves. For these services, personal managers often get a commission of 15 to 20 percent of your earnings, sometimes more depending on the extent of the services the manager is offering.

Note that, in both agent and manager agreements, compensation is typically calculated based on the artist's *gross earnings*. If you've got a deal in which there are going to be a lot of deductions from your gross—similar to the deductions discussed in the previous section about contracts in the recording industry—it's probably very wise to try to negotiate some exceptions to the gross earnings figure used to calculate the agent's or manager's commission.

It's also wise for the artist to have what's known as a *sunset clause* built into such contracts. You see, agents and managers will insist that your agreement include a provision stating that, even after the agreement is terminated, they will still be entitled to their commissions from work attained by you during the term of the contract. It's only fair. If someone puts time and effort into making an artist a marketable talent and getting him a paying gig, it wouldn't be right for that artist to allow the agent/manager agreement to expire before the job was done and then not pay the commission his agent or manager had earned for getting him that job. However, while fairness is a good thing, you probably wouldn't want to be paying top dollar for the rest of your life to someone you're no longer working with for a job he got you once upon a time. Therefore, a sunset clause is often negotiated by the artist to limit the amount of compensation an agent or manager gets following the termination of their contract. It might look something like this:

Notwithstanding anything to the contrary contained herein, the Manager's rate of commission payable by the Artist under this agreement for contracts entered into during the term of this agreement that are performed or exploited after the expiration or termination of the term of this agreement shall be payable as follows:

(a) *In the first year following the expiration or termination of the term (the "First Post-Term Period"), 20 percent with respect to personal appearances, and 15 percent with respect to all other entertainment industry income;*

(b) *In the second year following the expiration or termination of the term (the "Second Post-Term Period"), 15 percent with respect to personal appearances and 10 percent with respect to all other entertainment industry income; and*

(c) *In the third year following the expiration or termination of the term (the "Third Post-Term Period"), 10 percent with respect to personal appearances and 5 percent with respect to all other entertainment industry income.*

Notwithstanding anything to the contrary contained herein, no commission shall be payable to the Manager pursuant to this clause after the expiration of the Third Post-Term Period.

The term of an agent or manager contract usually takes the form of an initial contract period followed by options that allow the agent or manager to extend it. This is similar to the options that are typical in recording contracts. However, because of the time investment a manager might need to put into establishing a new artist, the initial contract period for a personal management agreement might be longer than is usual for a recording agreement—probably at least two years duration.

Sometimes bad things happen to good people, and relationships have been known to sour, whether they're personal or professional relationships. If you're an artist who finds yourself in a bad relationship with an agent or manager, you don't want to have to tough it out with that person longer than necessary just because you've signed a contract. In the end, a business agreement is supposed to be a benefit to both parties. So it's strongly recommended that the artist engaging the services of an agent or manager try to negotiate an escape clause, sometimes known as a *kick-out clause*. The basis of the escape clause is that the artist will be able to terminate the contract if the agent or manager doesn't fulfill some express condition or level of performance. The easiest measure is probably a predetermined earnings requirement within a set period of time. For example, the escape clause could state that:

> *If, after the first year following the execution of this agreement, the Artist's gross earnings from the exploitation of his art do not exceed $100,000, the artist may terminate this agreement by notifying the Manager in writing of such termination.*

Yes, it's sad when a relationship goes bust. Parting is such sweet sorrow—and oftentimes not so sweet. But think of the kick-out clause as a safety net. If the arrangement with a manager or agent isn't working out, it's probably best just to take the advice of the Paul Simon song that says "get yourself free."

Performance Outlets

Regardless of what the specific discipline might be, there's one thing that every artist in the performing arts absolutely, positively, no-doubt-about-it needs—*a place to perform*. This could take the form of a stage, a hall, a club, a public square, or any other venue, no matter how grand or modest, that affords the opportunity for the artist to present creative work before an audience. If you're a performing artist, or an artist who creates works for performers, the times may come when you have to negotiate the placement of your art in a particular venue. That being the case, once again we must take out our pens and be ready to sign yet another agreement—this time with whomever manages the performance outlet.

First, we must make note of the distinction that exists between a simple *venue for rent* and a *producing company*. A venue for rent is just a space that's leased for a period of time. The owners of the property may have no connection whatsoever to the business of art, and, as such, may have nothing to offer you in the way of necessary licenses, permits, insurance, or the like. Those are things the renters will be expected to supply for themselves, and you can probably expect to see a very explicit clause about it in the rental contract. If, for example, you're going to stage a dance concert at a rented venue, you'll be responsible for attaining all licenses or permissions necessary to sell tickets and admit an audience. In contrast, if a dance company hires you to choreograph or perform in its own production of a dance revue, the expectation is that the company will secure all necessary permissions because it's serving as the producing entity. In the end, it's the producer who typically bears the responsibility for ensuring that all the legalities have been properly attended.

The same holds true for a production of any type of performance where intellectual property permissions are required. Take, for example, a situation in which a playwright contracts with a theater company to have his play produced. The playwright, as the copyright owner, would sign a contract with the company to license the production rights. However, the playwright cannot sell more than he owns, and, if the play calls for the inclusion of someone else's copyright protected song, that will require that the grand performance rights to the song be attained—not necessarily by the playwright but, rather, by the theater company as the producer. If the theater company can't get the rights to the song, or refuses to pay for those rights, it doesn't get to use it in the show, regardless of what the script calls for or the playwright wants.

As regards this sort of responsibility, concert venues could go either way. Sometimes the venue is merely a space for rent, in which the artists are responsible for attaining the rights to use any music they, themselves, didn't write. Other times, the venue's operator is deemed to be the producer, such as those occasions when a bar hires a band to play live music. The bar will have to secure and pay for the small performing rights licenses administered by ASCAP, BMI, and SESAC if it wants that band to have the widest range of possibilities for its musical selection. Having a license with only one of the performing rights societies would entitle that bar to allow the band to play only those songs controlled by that particular society. Every other license-controlled song would be off limits. That restriction could even include the band's own original music if it's licensed by a society with which the bar doesn't have a license.

Ordinarily, in situations where the producer is traditionally expected to be responsible for such things, the performers are unlikely to be held liable for licensing or copyright violations. The copyright holder isn't likely to sue the actor who was directed to sing a copyright protected song in a certain scene in a show. It's not the actor's job to secure the rights to the material being presented, and it's unlikely any court would rule that it was. However, it would be an entirely different story if a performer is hired to do a show, and the hiring party—whom we'll call the "buyer"—requires that the performer warrant that he has attained permission to use all materials that are part of that performance. The buyer might insist on contract language such as:

> *The Artist, at his sole cost, shall obtain all licenses, permits, certificates, authorizations, or other approvals required to enable the performance to be performed in accordance with the terms of this agreement.*

The buyer might further require that the performer indemnify the buyer against any damages the buyer suffers as a result of the performer misrepresenting that he had the necessary permissions. Going back to our example of the theater company producing a play that calls for a copyright protected song, if the playwright falsely represents to the company that the playwright either owns the copyright to the song or has already secured permission for its use in the show, then the theater company will have grounds to sue the playwright for that misrepresentation should the company later find itself at the bad end of a copyright infringement lawsuit. Deliberate fraud that causes someone else to suffer damages is always a punishable offense.

Film, Television, and Radio

Since the 20th century, film, television, and radio have practically been the poster children of the commercial entertainment industry. How could they not be? It's not that other types of entertainment are perceived to be lesser forms, or are less appreciated or enjoyed. It's just that, when people dream about *making it big* in the biz, oftentimes their dreams drift toward thoughts of selling that blockbuster movie script, or landing that major role on a hit TV show, or hosting a coast-to-coast syndicated radio program, or something like that where there's big, big money involved, and an artist could earn a living just by doing that (as opposed to those of us who spend significant portions of our lives being lawyers so we can afford to eat while we indulge and subsidize our artistic passions). There's no secret that the *big three* are where the megabucks are—or, at least, where they are, potentially, for some. The fact is that most people working in these businesses aren't making anywhere near as much as you probably think they are. That's because you only hear about the monster deals for the superstars. *Variety* isn't going to run a front page headline that reads:

Screenwriter Options Script for $5,000

That's the sort of thing that makes people mutter, "Big whoop," and so it never makes the news. Whereas, you'd definitely hear about a headline that said something like:

Collector Buys Madonna's Toenail Clippings for $10 Million

And then you'd start thinking to yourself how you'd like to be famous so you, too, could sell your toenail clippings, even if just for half that amount.

Well, the bumpy road to fame and fortune isn't getting any less bumpy as I dawdle. So let's get to it and take a brief look at just a few of the many types of contracts an artist might encounter when dealing with these high profile media.

Since very little could be produced without some form of scripting, a logical starting point would be a look at *literary options* and *purchase agreements*. A literary option is a very common way for a script to be marketed to a producer. It's a way for a producer to buy and hold onto the rights to a literary property for a certain period of time during which that producer has the exclusive option to purchase it outright. Options are used to give the producer a chance to shop the project around, determine the level of interest others might have in it, and raise the money needed to produce it. The Writers Guild of America suggests that a literary option be purchased from a "professional writer" for no less than 10 percent of its recommended minimum purchase price, and that the duration of the option be for a period of up to 18 months.[56] During the term of the option agreement, the writer cannot offer the script to any other producer. Naturally, the more valuable the property, the more money the writer can demand for taking it off the open market while the producer decides whether or not to pursue the project. If the producer doesn't exercise the option, or renew it with the writer's permission (and probably another check to the writer), then the literary property reverts to the writer who keeps the option money and is free to market the script elsewhere.

In virtually all circumstances, such a literary option agreement is also simultaneously a literary purchase agreement. It specifies the conditions for

---

56   For more details about recommended script pricing, go to the Writers Guild's website at www.wga.org.

the outright purchase of the property—should the producer choose to exercise the option and pursue the project—and it includes all the provisions that go along with that, such as the full purchase price, whether the author gets first crack at doing any revisions to the script, and whether the author participates in a percentage of the gross profits of the project or any ancillary markets (such as other media, merchandising, etc.). Once the producer exercises the option, the purchase part of the agreement takes effect immediately.

Don't expect a producer merely to purchase a *license* for a script. With the amount of money at stake at this level, most producers will insist on buying the script outright with all rights attached. No producer wants to have a project held hostage by a writer who won't consent to a necessary revision. Most professional Hollywood writers long ago made their peace with the notion that you often just have to cash the check and hold your nose when the project is finally released with all the "fixes" that have been made to the original script.

However, even if the option has been exercised and the script sold in its entirety, a writer might still possess the ability to get the property back—that is, if the writer negotiated into the contract a reversion clause. Often such a clause is used to allow the writer to reclaim the property after a period of inactivity. Possible contract language might be something like:

> *If the Producer fails to actively develop the property within five (5) years of exercising the option under this agreement, the Writer will have, upon notifying the Producer in writing, the option to reacquire the property.*

The specifics of such a reacquisition would likely involve returning some or all of the money the writer was paid for the purchase of the script. Sorry about that, but reacquisition has its costs. If you can negotiate a better deal, good for you.

One of the big contract issues for writers involves *attribution* or, as it's usually referred to in the industry, *credit*. This is an especially thorny issue in the movies, where a script may go through so many hands and undergo so many collaborative changes that the original author may no longer be able to recognize his own work. There have been many occasions in the past where the original author's name has disappeared from the credits entirely. To deal with this, the Writers Guild has an arrangement with companies that sign onto its minimum basic agreement. That agreement allows the Guild to be the one that makes the determinations as to who gets writing credits for the script.

There's a line of dialogue from the film *Sunset Boulevard* in which a character says, "Audiences don't know somebody sits down and writes a picture—they think the actors make it up as they go along." And so it is that many of even the best writers in the industry toil in anonymity while many of those referred to as the "talent" are household names who command big salaries. For the talent, this can be both a blessing and a curse on so many different levels. Let's look at an example of one such mixed blessing.

We'll say that Linda is a big movie star—the type one considers "money in the bank" if she appears in a picture. We'll also say she has been signed to play the lead in a big-budget Western. Investors plunk down large sums of cash on the creditworthiness of Linda's name being attached to the project. However, before shooting begins, Linda's agent tells her about a rival studio that wants her to star in its own Western film. Linda announces she's pulling out of the first project, and—contract or no contract—she won't do the first movie because she'll be acting in the rival studio's film instead. Looking at it from a purely business standpoint, talent like Linda (and also some other highly recognizable people such as directors) are specialized artists who are contracted to perform very special and unique services. You don't just put an ad in the paper to fill the job of one of these people. Therefore, if Linda breaches her contract by refusing to do the first Western, and the investors sue her for that breach, the damage she has caused the project's investors might not be fully compensated with a simple award of cash. First, it's extremely difficult and speculative to estimate what the actual monetary loss will be for the investors, who were counting on Linda's celebrity to be a major element of the film's marketing. One might guess based on past experience, but that's still just a guess. Second, no one can say for certain what Linda's appearance in a rival Western being released at about the same time will do to the box office receipts for the first Western, which will be forced to have its lead recast with perhaps a less popular actor. The only way to know absolutely what value Linda's participation would have had for the first Western would be to actually make the picture with her in the lead role. But a court will not order someone to perform work in order to fulfill a contract. That's a little too much like indentured servitude for our Constitution. Yet, as an alternative, a court could issue an injunction forbidding someone who breaches an employment contract from working for a competitor during the term of the breached contract. In our example, the court might order Linda, in addition to paying monetary damages, also not to act in the competing Western.

Child actors and other very young performers raise a special concern regarding employment contracts. A child under the age of seven can't legally enter into a contract. Only a parent or legal guardian can do that on behalf of the child. What's more, even with the parent/guardian's authorization, a minor might be able to repudiate a contract up till the time that child turns 18. Because of this, in some cases, those who have contracted with child entertainers have taken the precaution of petitioning a court to make a determination as to whether the agreement is fair to the child. Getting such "pre-approval" from a court can make it more difficult for the child to disaffirm the contract later.

Another important element of the industry is music. In fact, it's no secret that music is huge in all three media—film, television, and radio. Heck, even during the silent era of motion pictures, the movies weren't viewed in silence. They'd have someone in the theater playing a piano to accompany the actions on the screen.

Having one's music incorporated into film, television, or radio programming can be quite lucrative. So it's often deemed to be a plum contract for the music artist. Such deals might come in the form of an agreement to use already existing music, or they might be deals that commission new compositions specifically for a project, such as an assignment to score the soundtrack of a movie. If it's the latter, there's a good chance the commissioning party will have a desire to head off any possible complications for himself by having the contract state that the composing artist is either an employee or an independent contractor creating a work made for hire. (Remember that, if either of those is the case, the commissioning party automatically owns the copyright on whatever music is created.)

Even where the commissioning party contracts to own the copyright outright, the composer will likely want to negotiate a clause into the agreement that provides that the composer will share in the proceeds should one or more of the songs later be published or used on a soundtrack album. If the artist already has an exclusive publishing and/or recording agreement with another company, an arrangement will have to be worked out between all the companies that have a contractual claim on the artist's work. Complicated, I realize, but necessary.

Then there could be times when an artist will be asked to compose music that *might be*, but not necessarily *will be*, used in a project. A fledgling composer could write the music on the speculation that it might be purchased (known as writing *on spec*), and then only receive payment if the music is actually used. But it would be nice if the artist got at least something for his effort, regardless of whether the producer actually ends up using the music. Therefore, under such circumstances, it might benefit the artist to negotiate what's called a *step deal* in which the commissioning party pays the composer something upfront with the guarantee that, if the commissioner then decides to actually use the music, the composer will be paid additional money. Sample contract language might look something like this:

> *The Producer agrees to pay the Artist $500 to compose and orchestrate an original song suitable to the project as described herein. If that song, or any recognizable part of it, is subsequently incorporated into the project in any way, form, or manner, the Producer shall pay the Artist an additional $4,500.*

Of course, film, TV, and radio are highly collaborative media, and it's possible that multiple people could be commissioned to do essentially the same work. For example, there may be several actors playing roles of similar importance. In such cases, each of the artists would probably like to know that what he's receiving is fair when compared to what the others are getting. There's nothing that says a hiring party has to compensate all similar artists the same way. But artists with some sway might be able to negotiate what's often called a *most favored nations clause* that guarantees them contract terms that are at least as good as those given to any other artist performing the same function on the project. If you can get it, a most favored nations clause is good to have. And I probably don't have to twist your arm to get you to agree with me there. Well, hey, if you've got as much talent and notoriety as the next guy, it's only fair that you ought to get at least as much as he does. Right? Contracts are supposed to be fair. Right? And life's always fair. Right?...

Right?...

Uh...*Ahem*...Hey, why don't we go back to talking about art...

What Happens to Art When the Artist No Longer Possesses It?

At some point in every parent's life, there comes a day when that parent must wave good-bye from the front door to the offspring who are marching off to make their own way in the world. It's the natural order of things. We give them life. We nurture them. We share our wisdom. And then, just when they get to the point where they can exit the house without instantly hurting themselves, they leave us. *Go raise children!*

Art is the birth child of every artist. It is born of creativity, ingenuity, and labor. Furthermore, once it has been born, it takes on a life of its own—a life that, in many ways, is separate from that of its creator and, if given a chance, can outlive that creator. All things that we create will, if they endure, eventually belong to someone else. Gracing our world today is art that has been left to us by people who lived perhaps hundreds, if not thousands, of years ago; art the exact origins of which might not always be discernible, but the beauty, meaning, and impact of which remain as fresh as if it had been unveiled only this moment. That's the legacy of the artist—to touch even those whom the artist may never personally meet.

In this, the last chapter of this book, we'll examine some legal issues and concepts that pertain to art once it has left the artist's possession.

First Sale Doctrine and *Droit de Suite*

Early in this text, we discussed the fact that the property rights to a work of art can be subdivided into as many distinct pieces as the artist can devise. The artist is then free to license or assign each of those pieces to other people. Licensing rights is the equivalent of *leasing* them. Just like our earlier comparison to a landlord leasing an apartment to a tenant, the artist never relinquishes ownership of the rights, he only licenses their use.

Assigning rights, on the other hand, amounts to an outright transfer of property, similar to selling a house. Once the deal is closed, the seller gives up all claims of ownership to the buyer.

However, be that as it may, it's still perfectly legal for someone to sell a home while retaining certain rights to the real estate on which the house is located. An example of this would be an *easement* in which the seller retains the right to have access to a portion of the land. Let's suppose, for illustration purposes, that you're selling Gary a piece of real estate, which is located directly in front of the lot where your home is located. The only way for you to get in and out of your lot is through the piece of property that Gary's buying. Naturally, a piece of land would be worthless to you if you couldn't get in or out of it. So, to ensure the utility and value of your home, you could sell Gary the front lot while retaining an easement that allows you to cross Gary's lot for the purpose of accessing the outside roads. Your having an easement through the land doesn't take away Gary's right to use and call the entire piece of real estate his property. It just means that there's a retained right of access that you possess on that lot, and, legally, Gary can't infringe that right by forbidding your access or putting up a fence that blocks your way.

Virtually any type of property (real estate or otherwise) can be sold with the seller retaining certain rights, provided both the seller and buyer agree to the terms. That includes works of art, even where the physical substance of the art changes hands and leaves the artist's possession forever. If the artist wishes to reserve certain privileges related to the art, the artist is free to offer its sale with the caveat that those particular rights are reserved by the artist. That's generally done either by explicitly retaining the rights (e.g., *"The Artist expressly reserves the right to make duplicate copies of the art and to distribute those copies to others for sale in the open retail market."*), or by explicitly assigning only specific rights that implicitly retain all others (e.g., *"The Artist expressly assigns to the Buyer the non-exclusive right to sell the art in the open retail market but not the right to make or distribute duplicate copies of the art."*).

Despite this, there are limits to the artist's reach in terms of controlling what happens to a piece of art once it has been sold. Under something called the *first sale doctrine*, once a piece has been legally sold to another, the artist cannot then dictate the terms of any further sales of that particular piece. To illustrate, suppose that Dawn writes mystery novels. Patrick buys one of Dawn's novels in a chain bookstore, reads it, and then takes it to a local used book shop to sell it. Dawn cannot prevent Patrick from selling the book to the used book shop, nor can she stop that shop from reselling the book on the open market for whatever value that shop feels it's worth. Dawn's ability to control to whom and how a copy of her book is sold is limited to the first sale of that copy. Any subsequent sales of that copy are beyond her powers. Nor can Dawn claim she's entitled to a share of the money derived from the resale of that copy of her book. Her right to benefit economically from that copy ended after the first sale transferred ownership of it to someone else. No matter how many times that copy may be resold, Dawn will never see another dime from it.

If that seems somehow inherently unfair to you, perhaps you'll like a doctrine known as *droit de suite*. In its basic legal definition, *droit de suite* involves a creditor's right to chase a debtor's property that falls into a third party's hands. In Europe, this doctrine was crafted into a justification for giving creators of fine art a legal right to receive compensation from sales of their art that occur following the first sale. To give an example, let's say Erin is a painter, and she sells a work to a collector for $1,000. Three years later, the value of her painting skyrockets to $20,000. The collector then resells the painting and pockets $19,000 profit. The only thing the collector did to earn this kind of windfall was to have the foresight—or just sheer luck—to have purchased Erin's painting when it was a veritable steal. Meanwhile, for all the talent and labor that went into creating the now valuable work, Erin profited only $1,000, minus her costs. Those who support *droit de suite* say that the artist ought to get something more than just a pat on the back when her art is later resold; and, where the legal doctrine is recognized, the artist would, indeed, be legally entitled to a small percentage of the proceeds of subsequent sales.

Statutory *droit de suite* traces its origin to France in the 1920s, and other countries have since adopted it. In the United States, only California has some statutory form of a *droit de suite* law[57], and, among its restrictions, it applies only to fine art that is either sold in that state or where the seller of the art resides there.

Droit Moral

Going back to this chapter's introductory metaphor, among a mother's or father's greatest fears when a child leaves the parental nest is the worry that some evil will befall that child—something the absent parent will be

---

57   California Civil Code § 986.

unable to prevent. This, too, is a genuine concern of the artist who sells his art and, in so doing, places it in the hands of others whom the artist cannot control. A buyer might not think twice about making modifications to a work of art he has purchased. The assumption of the buyer is often that, since he now owns the art, he's entitled to do with it whatever he pleases. After all, if you buy a car, the manufacturer can't forbid you from driving it in a demolition derby, despite the terrible toll such an activity will likely take on the auto. It's your car, and you can do what you want with it—including wrecking it. The auto manufacturer might not even mind since, once the car is wrecked, you might be in the market for a new one it could then sell you.

However, the artist who takes pride in his work (and feels his art is something more representative of his artistic self than might be a mass produced commodity) may feel more than a slight twinge of pain if he learns that a buyer has mutilated or distorted his art. Once a work of art has been modified by someone other than the artist, it could be said that it no longer properly represents the artist's true talent. Instead, the modified work might represent someone else's talent or, possibly even worse for the artist, misrepresent the artist's abilities and give a false impression that would cause people to view the artist in a detrimental light. This is a highly sensitive area for artists who value their reputation, and it led some places to adopt a protective doctrine known as *droit moral*, or "moral rights" of the artist.

Droit moral was another innovation of French law. In jurisdictions recognizing the *droit moral* doctrine, even after a work has left the artist's possession and has been legally acquired by someone else, the artist still has the right to object to distortions, mutilations, or other modifications that would be prejudicial to the author's honor or reputation. This doctrine was a part of the Berne Convention of 1971, in which most nations of the world agreed to certain standards of international copyright protections. Although the United States was one of the Berne Convention nations, the U.S. Congress has never seen fit to pass a specific law equivalent to the *droit moral* section of the Berne Convention. Instead, the United States has adhered to the philosophy that artistic moral rights already exist in America under such laws as the Lanham Act and common law rules against misrepresentation.

Remember the case of *Gilliam v. American Broadcasting Companies*? That was the case, discussed in an earlier chapter, where the creators of *Monty Python's Flying Circus* sued ABC for the unauthorized editing the network did to the plaintiffs' TV show. In its ruling, the court noted that U.S. copyright law did not recognize moral rights, and the Copyright Act did not provide a particular statutory ground for a lawsuit making that allegation. However, the court added,

> *Nevertheless, the economic incentive for artistic and intellec-*
> *tual creation that serves as the foundation for American copy-*
> *right law...cannot be reconciled with the inability of artists to*
> *obtain relief for mutilation or misrepresentation of their work to*
> *the public on which the artists are financially dependent.*

Based on the significant and detrimental distortions the Pythons' show suffered at the hands of ABC's editing choices, the court concluded that "the edited broadcast by ABC impaired the integrity of the [Pythons'] work and represented to the public as the product of [the Pythons] what was actually a mere caricature of their talents." *Droit moral* statutes, or no *droit moral* statutes, the court ruled in the Pythons' favor.

Those battling the computerized colorization of black-and-white movies weren't so successful. After years of championing a cause to keep black-and-white motion pictures just as they were originally shot, film artists were never able to get Congress to pass a moral rights law to prohibit colorization. If you see less colorization of old movies taking place these days, it's because the practice has mostly gone out of vogue, not because there's any law against it.

The Copyright Act's first genuine moral rights clause was added in 1990 as Section 106A, known as the *Visual Artists Rights Act*. This amendment is applicable, and specifically limited, to visual arts such as paintings, sculpture, sketches, still photographs, and the like. It allows the artist two types of moral rights: the *right of integrity* and the *right of attribution*.

The right of integrity embodied in the act allows the artist to prevent any intentional mutilation or distortion of his work where that mutilation or distortion would be prejudicial to the artist's honor or reputation. It also gives the artist the right to prevent any destruction, either intentional or through gross negligence, of art that the act describes as "a work of recognized stature." Michelangelo's statue of David is undoubtedly a work of recognized stature. Whether your art meets the definition is something that might be up to interpretation and the subject of debate. But you get the idea of what the act is talking about.

The right of attribution has to do with the artist's right (1) to claim authorship of the work he created, (2) to prevent his name being misapplied to a work he did not create, and (3) to prevent his name being used in connection with art he did create if that art has been distorted, mutilated, or otherwise modified such that it would be prejudicial to the honor or reputation of the artist.

In addition to that federal law, some states have also enacted moral rights laws to protect the rights of visual artists. The rights and restrictions may vary from state to state.

Artist Estate Planning

If you're planning to live forever, you can skip this part. For the rest of us, it's time to have that little heart-to-heart chat about what's to become of our stuff once we have succumbed to that other inevitability that *isn't* paying taxes.

Everyone should have a will or a living trust that spells out that person's exact wishes for how possessions are to be distributed to surviving heirs. It may not be the most cheerful topic, contemplating one's own mortality. But it's a genuine kindness to the people you love to make these decisions in advance so that they don't later have to guess or debate over what you really wanted.

Many artists are under the impression that, if they haven't earned much money from their labors, they haven't much to leave their heirs. So they conclude that a will or trust would be an unnecessary bother and expense. However, this kind of thinking overlooks one very important fact. An artist's estate isn't composed solely of that person's money and various personal effects. It also includes the *art* that person has created and maintains some control over—and that also means all *copyrights* in the artist's possession. Remember that a copyright, with all its various rights and privileges, lasts another seventy years after the artist's death. Whatever intellectual property the artist owns at the time of death is a property that can be bequeathed to that artist's heirs. Intellectual property is, after all, *property*, just like a house, a car, furniture, or a cherished family heirloom handed down from generation to generation. After a lifetime of creating works that figuratively represent the heart and soul of the artist, it would be nothing short of a shame for that artist to have his work lost to mishandling or neglect due to a simple lack of planning. Therefore, I encourage every artist to do yourself and future generations the favor of undertaking a little estate planning for your art.

The first thing an artist should do is to make a complete inventory of all the art in that artist's possession, including any rights that have been retained in works that were sold; and, conversely, the artist should also note any specific rights that have been granted to others—this so that heirs don't end up waging losing battles over rights they only thought they possessed. It's important to all estate planning that the records reflect accurately what is and isn't part of the estate. Also very helpful to include in that inventory is the location of the art, if it's not obvious. Such an inventory might look something like the following example:

SAMPLE ARTIST INVENTORY

Title	Date	Description	Copyright Reg. No.	Rights Granted/Reserved	Location
Mona Leta	1998	Oil painting on canvas, 18" x 24"	VA??????	Sold to Waldo Whatzit, 1999. Copyright reserved.	Whatzit Gallery, Wheredhego, Maryland
The Last Brunch	1999	Commissioned mural, 20' x 9'		Work made for hire. Retained attribution right.	Saint Bluto's Church, Sweltering Creek, Utah
Naked Guy in a Circle and Square	2000	Pen and ink sketch, 10" x 10"	VA??????	Public display rights licensed to Brainiac Think Tank through December 31, 2035. All other rights reserved.	Brainiac Think Tank, Egghead, Indiana
Knock Off Art for Fun and Profit	2001	Non-fiction book	TX??????	Published by Rundown House, 2002. 12% royalties on invoice price.	Publishing contract kept in safe deposit box #530, Megabucks Bank, 13 Wealthy St., Weasel Falls, Vermont
My Career as a Knock Off Artist	2002	Non-fiction book	TX??????	Unpublished. All rights reserved.	Manuscript and digital copies kept in home office filing cabinet.

The above is only a sample, and your own inventory could contain much more information if you feel it's necessary. While making the inventory, just think to yourself that what you want this inventory to tell your heirs or executors is (1) what's in your estate, (2) how to find it, and (3) what can be done with it.

Regardless of whether the artist uses a will, a living trust, or some other legal instrument to bequeath possessions, it's crucial that the artist make a clear statement of exactly what he wants done with his art after his death. If the artist wants a particular piece to go to a particular heir, it should say so specifically. If the artist wishes a piece to be destroyed following his death, that, too, should be specified. If a work is to be shared by multiple heirs, it should state whether all rights are being shared equally—including control of the property—or whether some rights are being left to only one person.

Suppose, for example, that Bill is a playwright. If they are popular plays, his dramas will likely continue to be produced long after Bill has shuffled off this mortal coil. He wants all his children to benefit equally from any royalties or other monies the plays generate. However, the only child he feels has the business acumen to properly manage the bookings, production contracts, and potential subsidiary rights is his daughter, Marian. As such, Bill specifies in his will that, while all of his offspring are left an equal share in the economic interests of his plays, Marian is appointed the *literary executor* who will, upon her father's death, possess the sole powers for any decisions related to his dramatic works.

A literary or art executor manages only the art portion of an estate. The remainder of the estate is managed by a general executor or personal representative. In some cases, this division of responsibilities is done because, while the artist may trust the executor of his estate to carry out the necessary legal tasks involving such things as money, real estate, and personal effects, the artist might also want to ensure that the person who makes the decisions as to what is to become of the estate's art is someone who shares or, at least, understands the artist's aesthetic vision and will preserve or enhance the artist's reputation. However, there could be times when a decision made by a literary or art executor might come into conflict with a decision made by the general executor of the estate. Such a situation might arise if portions of the estate's art need to be sold to pay estate debts or taxes. The general executor and the art executor might not see eye to eye on such a decision, and the result could be a financially dangerous stalemate for the estate and its intended beneficiaries. To avoid this, the particular duties and powers of the art executor need to be specified in the will, as well as a provision that expresses whose decision will take priority—that of the art executor or that of the general executor—in the event of a dispute.

There are a few things that should be taken into account when an artist bequeaths his art to others. For one thing, copyrights are crucial elements that must be specifically addressed in a will or trust if they are meant to be transferred to a specific heir. Keep in mind that a copyright is not automatically transferred with the physical possession of a property. Merely leaving your printed photographs and their negatives to a friend, for example, doesn't convey the right for that friend now to make copies and market them. In death, as in life, to assign a copyright to someone, it must be specified *in a signed writing* that you are doing so. So don't forget to include that in your will.

The same is true for any special instructions you have for the financial benefits that might go along with an intellectual property. Going back to our above example, if Bill wants Marian to inherit all his literary works, as well as the copyrights attached to them and the financial benefits derived from them, he might express that in his will with language that goes something like:

> *I bequeath to my daughter, Marian, all of my literary properties, including, but not limited to, all copyrights in those works and any royalties or other monies derived from them.*

With this type of specificity, Marian takes possession not only of any physical copies of the play scripts, but she also takes possession of the same rights her father had to control the exploitation of the plays and benefit financially from them. If the will doesn't specify who gets the copyrights and the financial benefits, then those might be deemed to be *intestate property*—that is, property that was not addressed by, and isn't passed on by the will. In such cases, intestate property is passed to whomever that state's laws say is next in line for inheritance. In this case, that might be Bill's wife, who may or may not be a person Bill would approve of having the copyrights and financial benefits that go along with his work.

Another thing to think about in estate planning is the tax considerations that might be applicable. Sometimes an artist will bequeath a work to a charitable organization with the intention that the donation will be a deduction to offset estate taxes. The thing to keep in mind there is that, if the art being donated doesn't have a related use to what the receiving organization does, the donation may not be tax deductible. Donating a sculpture to an animal shelter might be a nice gesture, but the shelter's business doesn't connect in any realistic way to the art. Therefore, it would be difficult to make the case that the donated statue amounted to a valuable addition to the shelter's particular charitable purpose, and the IRS might not allow the deduction.[58]

It's also important to note that, for a donation of a work of art to qualify for a tax deduction, that donation must also include the accompanying copyright. If you maintain the copyright on a donated work, you haven't fully parted with that work or its potential value. If you haven't given up the value, you don't get to deduct it from Uncle Sam.

Additionally, you have to understand that, just because you want someone to have something of yours, it doesn't mean that person has to accept it. Upon my death, I'd really like to have my literary works put on public display in the Library of Congress, but, unless I acquire in my lifetime a sufficient degree of fame as a writer, having my works displayed there is not exactly an odds-on favorite. The artist who wishes to bequeath his work to renowned museums, libraries, archives, and such, needs to pause for a reality check. Ask yourself if these institutions know you and your work. Ask yourself if they're in the habit of accepting such art from people like you. If you can't answer for certain, then contact the institution and ask if it would accept what you're offering. If it won't, then leaving it to that institution will only result in that work of art being deemed intestate property and passing into the hands of some other heir—possibly one whom you, yourself, wouldn't approve of acquiring it. (My art in the hands of a Philistine? Would that be a fate worse than death?)

The fact is that anyone can refuse a bequeathed gift. If you haven't specified an alternate recipient in the event of refusal, that gift will then be passed on according to your state's laws of intestate succession. So, before you go divvying up the goodies in your will, you might just want to check with those people to be sure, first, that they'll accept, and, second, that they'll do with the art what you'd like to see done with it. Of course, you won't be around to make absolutely certain they're not using your masterpiece oil painting as a tablecloth at your funeral. But the chances for your desires

---

58   This tax rule is governed by Internal Revenue Code § 2055(e)(4).

coming true are much better if you get to select, by a legally enforceable document, where your art goes.

And that, my friends, is why the law was invented—to create a working structure by which we can all agree how things are supposed to proceed. Once you've got the legalities nailed down, you can breathe a sigh of contentment while you hear yourself saying:

"I take comfort in knowing that what I possess will go to those I want to have it."…

"Except for the brown sticks! Those you're giving back to me!"
"No way! They were green when I took 'em!"
"Well, they're brown now!"
"Talk to the hand, sweetheart!"
"Talk to my lawyer, bucko!"…

Ah!—you've just gotta love the law!

Resources

Amada, Richard, *Elvis Karaoke Shakespeare and the Search for a Copyrightable Stage Direction*, 43 ARIZ. L. REV. 677 (2001), available online at *Arizona Law Review*, www.law.arizona.edu/Journals/ALR/ALR2001/content_v43n3.cfm

American Society of Composers, Authors and Publishers (ASCAP)
2675 Paces Ferry Road, SE
Suite 350
Atlanta, GA 30339
(800) 505-4052
www.ascap.com

Applying for 501(c)(3) Tax-Exempt Status, available online at Internal Revenue Service, www.irs.gov

Broadcast Music, Inc. (BMI)
320 West 57th St.
New York, NY 10019
(888) 689-5264
www.bmi.com

Catalogue of Copyright Entries, available at the U.S. Copyright Office and many major libraries

Dramatists Guild of America
    1501 Broadway
    Suite 701
    New York, NY 10036
    (212) 398-9366
    www.dramatistsguild.com

Harry Fox Agency, Inc.
    601 West 26th St.
    Suite 500
    New York, NY 10001
    (212) 834-0100
    www.harryfox.com

Federal Communications Commission
    445 12th Street, S.W.
    Washington, DC 20554
    (888) 225-5322
    www.fcc.gov

Riley, Peter Jason, *New Tax Guide for Writers, Artists, Performers, & Other Creative People* (Focus Publishing 2009)

SESAC (originally Society of European Stage Authors & Composers)
    5 Music Square East
    Nashville, TN 37203
    (615) 320-0055
    www.sesac.com

Stage Directors and Choreographers Society
    1501 Broadway
    Suite 1701
    New York, NY 10036
    (800) 541-5204
    www.sdcweb.org

United States Copyright Office
  101 Independence Ave., S.E.
  Washington, DC 20559-6000
  (202) 707-3000
  www.copyright.gov

United States Department of the Treasury
  Internal Revenue Service
  Washington, DC 20224
  (800) 829-1040
  www.irs.gov

United States Patent and Trademark Office
  P.O. Box 1450
  Alexandria, VA 22313-1450
  (800) 786-9199
  www.uspto.gov

Writers Guild of America, East
  555 W 57th St.
  New York, NY 10019
  (212) 767-7800
  www.wgaeast.org

Writers Guild of America, West
  7000 West Third Street
  Los Angeles, CA 90048
  www.wga.org

Case References

A&M Records v. Napster, 239 F.3d 1004 (9th Cir. 2001)
Bayer Co. v. United Drug Co., 272 F. 505 (S.D.N.Y. 1921)
Benny v. Loew's Inc., 239 F.2d 532 (9ᵗʰ Cir. 1956)
Blanch v. Koons, 467 F.3d 244 (2d Cir. 2006)
Bright Tunes Music Corp. v. Harrisongs Music, 420 F. Supp. 177 (S.D.N.Y. 1976)
Burrow-Giles Lithographic Co. v. Sarony, 111 U.S. 53 (1884)
Campbell v. Acuff-Rose Music, 510 U.S. 569 (1994)
Chaplin v. Amador, 93 Cal. App. 358 (1928)
Childress v. Taylor, 945 F.2d 500 (2d Cir. 1991)
Columbia Pictures Corp. v. National Broadcasting Co., 137 F. Supp. 348 (S.D. Cal. 1955)
Community for Creative Non-Violence v. Reid, 490 U.S. 730 (1989)
Detective Comics v. Bruns Publications, 111 F.2d 432 (2d Cir. 1940)
Elsmere Music v. National Broadcasting Company, 482 F. Supp 741 (S.D.N.Y. 1980)
Erickson v. Trinity Theatre, 13 F.3d 1061 (7th Cir. 1994)
Federal Communications Commission v. Pacifica Foundation, 438 U.S. 726 (1978)
Fisher v. Star Co., 231 N. Y. 414 (1921)
Gershwin Publishing Corp. v. Columbia Artists Management, 443 F.2d 1159 (2d Cir. 1971)
Gilliam v. American Broadcasting Companies, 538 F.2d 14 (2d Cir. 1976)
Haynes v. Alfred A. Knopf, 8 F.3d 1222 (7ᵗʰ Cir. 1993)
Hoehling v. Universal City Studios, 618 F.2d 972 (2nd Cir. 1980)
Jacobellis v. Ohio, 378 U.S. 184 (1964)
Miller v. California, 413 U.S. 15 (1973)

Murray v. National Broadcasting Company, 844 F.2d 988 (2d Cir. 1988)

Nash v. CBS, 899 F.2d 1537 (7th Cir. 1990)

Original Appalachian Artworks v. Cradle Creations, 223 U.S.P.Q. 80 (N.D. Ga. 1983)

Pruneyard Shopping Center v. Robins, 447 U.S. 74 (1980)

Raffles v. Wichelhaus, 2 Hurl. & C. 906 (Court of Exchequer 1864)

Russell v. Price, 612 F.2d 1123 (9th Cir. 1979)

Sheldon v. Metro-Goldwyn Pictures Corp., 81 F.2d 49 (2nd Cir. 1936)

Sony Corporation of America v. Universal City Studios, 464 U.S. 417 (1984)

Tempo Music, Inc. v. Famous Music Corp., 838 F. Supp. 162 (S.D.N.Y. 1993)

Thomson v. Larson, 147 F.3d 195, (2nd Cir. 1998)

Warner Brothers Pictures v. Majestic Pictures, *70 F.2d 310* (2nd Cir. 1934)

Warner Brothers v. American Broadcasting Companies, 720 F.2d 231 (2nd Cir. 1983)

Wendt v. Host International, 125 F.3d 806 (9th Cir. 1997)

White v. Samsung Electronics America, 971 F.2d 1395 (9th Cir. 1993)

Statutory References

Berne Convention for the Protection of Literary and Artistic Works
California Civil Code § 986
California Labor Code § 2855
Code of Federal Regulations, 37 C.F.R. § 201.20
Code of Federal Regulations, 37 C.F.R. § 202.1(a)
Copyright Act of 1909
Copyright Act of 1976, 17 U.S.C. § 101, *et seq.*
Digital Millennium Copyright Act
Internal Revenue Code § 501(c)(3)
Internal Revenue Code § 2055(e)(4)
Lanham Act, Section 43(a), codified as 15 U.S.C. § 1125(a)
Statute of Anne, 8 Anne, c. 19 (1709)
United States Bill of Rights
United States Code: Crimes and Criminal Procedure, 18 U.S.C. § 1461
United States Constitution, First Amendment
United States Constitution, Fourteenth Amendment
Uruguay Round Agreements Act of 1994
Visual Artists Rights Act, codified as 17 U.S.C. §106A

Index